L is for Lifestyle

L is for Lifestyle | *Ruth Valerio*

INTER-VARSITY PRESS
38 De Montfort Street, Leicester LE1 7GP, England
Email: ivp@ivpbooks.com
Website: www.ivpbooks.com

First published 2004
Reprinted 2005, 2006

British Library Caraloguing-in-Publication Data
A catalogue record for this book is available from the British Library.

ISBN-10: 1-84474-025-0
ISBN-13: 978-1-84475-025-3

Set in 9.5/13pt Rotis

Typeset in Great Britain by CRB Associates, Reepham, Norfolk

Printed and bound in Great Britain by Creative Print and Design (Wales),
Ebbw Vale

*Inter-Varsity Press publishes Christian books that are true to the Bible and
that communicate the gospel, develop discipleship and strengthen the church
for its mission in the world.*

*Inter-Varsity Press is closely linked with the Universities and Colleges
Christian Fellowship, a student movement connecting Christian Unions in
universities and colleges throughout Great Britain, and a member movement
of the International Fellowship of Evangelical Students.*
Website: www.uccf.org.uk

Contents

Foreword

At a UCCF leaders' conference in 1966, my wife Maggie attended a seminar on 'The Christian in society' led by Samuel Escobar. We still have the notes of that seminar. The concluding paragraph says, 'We have to preach the Gospel. We have to live the Gospel. It is not an either/or, but both are imperative.' That seminar was key for Maggie in putting social justice on her agenda, and its impact for both of us has been lifelong.

By the early seventies Maggie and I were being gently mocked by some friends as members of the 'muck and muesli brigade'. They told us that we came to mind when *The Good Life* was on the television – with some justification because by then we actually did have chickens in our back garden!

Compared to the wealth of excellent books on evangelism there are few on how we can be faithful to God in the most mundane aspects of our everyday lives. This is one of the few. It is a book about what it means to live as a Christian at the beginning of the twenty-first century. In essence it is a book about holiness, about how people who have devoted themselves to God should live under Jesus Christ's authority and guidance.

It has been written by someone who trusts Jesus as her personal Saviour and who longs that others should trust him as well, but who is also seeking to live in obedience to his

Word. Taking Jesus' authority over the life of the believer seriously, this book explores what the Bible has to say about how we shop, eat, invest, travel and so on. It is a book about offering our bodies, our earthly existence, as a sacrifice to God and refusing to be conformed to the pattern of this world in our daily living (Rom. 12:1–2). It challenges us to bring a whole range of different aspects of our everyday living under the authority of the Lord. I have no doubt that if we took it seriously, our neighbours would become much more willing to listen to our message.

The imaginative structure, passionate advocacy and comprehensive coverage of lifestyle issues in this volume belong to the author, but most of what she deals with is not new to evangelicals. For many of us whose spiritual formation took place in the late sixties and early seventies of the last century, there is here a fresh and vibrant reaffirmation of many things that we discovered then.

In 1980 the Lausanne Committee on World Evangelisation and the World Evangelical Fellowship (now called the World Evangelical Alliance), produced a statement entitled 'An Evangelical Commitment to Simple Lifestyle' (published in *Third Way*, June 1980). It still stands as a powerful support to the stance that is taken in this book. This commitment also emphasizes the inseparability of how we live from what we say:

> ... the call to responsible lifestyle must not be divorced from the call to responsible witness. For the credibility of our message is seriously diminished whenever we contradict it by our lives. It is impossible with integrity to proclaim Christ's salvation if he has evidently not saved us from greed, or his lordship if we are not good stewards of our possessions, or his love if we close our hearts against the needy. When Christians care for each other and for the deprived, Jesus Christ becomes more visibly attractive (p. 21).

The beauty of this book by Ruth Valerio is that it tells us how, consciously and practically, we can reject the values and standards of the world in favour of the values and standards of the kingdom of God. It is full of practical suggestions on how we can live our daily lives in a way that is more consistent with the will of God our Saviour. I am totally convinced that if an increasing number of us who call ourselves evangelical Christians took on board what is being advocated here in the way we live our lives, many more people would be asking us what they have to do to be saved. May God grant us such a Holy Spirit-induced revival of true Christianity. My prayer is that God will use this fresh and imaginative book to that end.

Dewi Hughes
Theological Advisor, Tearfund

Introduction

At a conference some time ago I was having dinner with a
fellow speaker and discussing the work I was doing with Cred
(Christian Relief, Education and Development). We were
reflecting together on the need to help people overcome the
inertia that so often results from being faced with huge global
problems. We discussed how to stimulate a realization of what
all of us can do to make a difference. At that time I was writing a
monthly 'Alphabet Lifestyle' column in the Cred newsletter,
giving regular updates on Cred's work and facilitating a network of people who want to use their lives to make a difference
in this world. As I told him about my aim for this column, I
suddenly realized that here was the outline for a book!

My own background is of a thoroughly Christian nature,
being raised on a good diet of prayer and Bible study, with an
emphasis on discipleship and personal evangelism, both local
and overseas. As I grew into adulthood, I met Christians who
were very active in their communities: running play-schemes
on the local estate, giving their time as local councillors,
working with the homeless and getting involved in environmental issues. At the same time, my husband was employed
by our church to teach on development education in schools,
and he was having his eyes opened to the realities of global
poverty and injustice. As I spent time with these friends I
began to see that they had a dimension to their Christian faith
that I was missing.

I went back to the Gospels to look at Jesus and saw that word and deed went together as Jesus travelled around, 'teaching in their synagogues, preaching the good news of the kingdom, and healing every disease and sickness' (Matt. 4:23 and 9:35; see also Acts 10:38). Jesus' message that the kingdom of God had come in his own person (Luke 11:20) called people to repent and follow him. Its focus was on the future fullness of God's kingdom, pictured as a rich banquet (e.g. Luke 14:15–24), but its outworking was to be immediate and related to people's physical as well as spiritual needs. Jesus' answer to the question as to whether or not he was 'the one who was to come' was to point to the results of his teaching and preaching: 'the blind receive sight, the lame walk, those who have leprosy are cured, the deaf hear, the dead are raised and the good news is preached to the poor' (Matt. 11:5). The influence of the kingdom of God reached into every aspect of people's lives, including the social and economic; the sign that salvation had come to Zacchaeus' house was that he gave half of his possessions to the poor and paid back fourfold all those he had cheated (Luke 19:8–9). Jesus' example showed me that I too needed to have compassion for people's physical needs while not losing the desire to see people repent and follow him.

This double-edged understanding of Jesus' ministry, and hence of our mission, is reflected in the documents that came out of the Lausanne Movement, which became definitive for almost all evangelical Christians around the world. In the middle of the twentieth century a significant portion of the evangelical wing of the church lost the social zeal for which it had become so well known in the previous two centuries.[1] The Lausanne Congress of 1974 was a milestone in bringing evangelism and social concern back together again. Paragraph 5 of the Lausanne Covenant, on Christian Social Responsibility, stated that they are 'both part of our Christian duty'. This statement was refined at the Consultation on the Relationship Between Evangelism and Social Responsibility in 1982. Here it was made clear that social responsibility is a consequence of evangelism, a bridge to evangelism and also a partner to evangelism.[2] This partnership was described as being like two blades of a pair of scissors, or, to change the metaphor, two wings of a bird. That bird is the bird of the gospel that unites both actions together: 'for the Gospel is the root, of which both evangelism and social responsibility are the fruits'.[3]

In 'A is for Activists' we shall look further at why we should be involved in what is going on in our world today – since some people may still ask why we need to be interested at all. Shouldn't we just be concerned with telling people about Jesus? *L is for Lifestyle* doesn't diminish the importance of that, but rather focuses on the 'social transformation' aspect of our overall mission and looks at how our lives can contribute to that particular dimension.[4]

Many Christians are deeply concerned with the problems of injustice and poverty that are so prevalent in our world. They recognize that their lives are interlinked with the lives of others around the world. They already give to various charities, but want to do more with their lifestyles to try to make those links beneficial rather than detrimental. The scale of the issues often seems overwhelming, however, leading to a sense of hopelessness. People do not know where to start.[5] This book aims to break the issues down into manageable, bite-sized chunks, and to give very practical pointers to how we can respond.

You may be new to these issues, and keen to learn more about what is happening and begin to take some first steps. You may be doing lots already and need some fresh ideas. You may be a student who wants to know what lifestyle options you can adopt when you graduate. You may want to know how you can juggle the demands of a young family and mortgage repayments and still be a Christian who is actively concerned with wider global issues. Perhaps you are well established in life, with children at university and a good income (and a matching credit-card bill!) coming in every month, and yet you still want to know how you can use the things God has blessed you with to bless others. You might now be retired, or maybe you have been made redundant, and you want to see how you can use your time to make a difference. Perhaps you are just exhausted with the pressures of consumerism and you want to explore the possibilities of a simpler lifestyle.

There are a host of different things we can do to make a difference, and this book gives suggestions for minor changes as well as major challenges. Whatever your situation, you will find things in this book to encourage and inspire you. Conversely, your particular situation may also mean that there are aspects of this book that you cannot take on. The aim is most definitely not to make you feel guilty! Try taking a step-by-step approach, doing one or two things first, rather than taking on all the action points at once. When they become a part of your normal life, then do some more. This is a book that you can come back to time and time again, dipping into different chapters as you wish.

It will be obvious as you read on that this book comes from my own journey through these issues. I have become increasingly aware of the problems that our world is facing, and concerned that, as a follower of Jesus, I have to play my part in doing something about them. The book therefore arises from my own circumstances – that is, normal life! I don't live up a mountain in total self-sufficiency; I live on a council estate with two young children, a mortgage, an ISA or two, and the stress of supermarket shopping. Lots of this book I am living already, and I hope I am an encouraging example of the fact that it can be done. There are parts of this book, though, where the suggested action is still an aspiration for me. There, the book reflects how I want to be living, rather than what I am doing already. For those of you who know me well, I ask you to be kind to me! Because it comes from my own journey, this book contains a lot of my personal opinions and stories. There will no doubt be things that you disagree with and other ways of achieving the ends I set out. My hope is that you will find your own way through the pointers that this book provides.

13

On a practical note, each chapter ends, where appropriate, with suggestions for further reading and organizations to contact. (The books listed, or cited in the Notes, appear with full publication details in the Bibliography at the end of the book.) By including these books and organizations I am not necessarily endorsing every aspect of them. Organizations can change their policies or campaigns and we may not agree with all they do. Again I would encourage you to do your own research on the issues and to use this book to help yourself to find your own path.

Because this book is aimed specifically at encouraging Christians to engage on a global level, I have included a large amount of biblical material to enable us to see how these things are an integral part of our faith. The amount of material varies from chapter to chapter (some chapters, such as 'C is for Creation' and 'M is for Money', contain a lot, while others, such as 'K is for Kippers' and 'O is for Organic', contain very little). I have deliberately tried to make each one read differently, rather than following a set structure, so that the chapters don't become boring.

I need to thank those people who have helped me with *L is for Lifestyle*. Roy McCloughry has given a great deal of his time to working through the manuscript with me, and to helping me, as a first-time author, to get the book into a publishable state. A massive 'thank you' to him. The Friends of the Earth Information Service has consistently replied to my questions with detailed and helpful answers. Thank you, also, to Tim Bushell, Michael Lomotey, Bev Thomas, and my parents Martin and Elizabeth Goldsmith, who all read through and commented on individual chapters.

Finally, this book is dedicated to my wonderful husband, Greg, who first opened my eyes to justice issues and pushed me constantly to write a book; and to my two children Mali and Jemba. May I inspire in them the love for God's world and his people that my parents inspired in me.

A is for Activists

One of my most memorable experiences was visiting the work
of the Sisters of Charity, Mother Teresa's order, in Addis   15
Ababa, Ethiopia. In that city of incredible poverty, their call is
to the very bottom of the heap: to those who are dying and
have been abandoned by friends and family. Each morning,
the sisters open the gates of their compound and bring in
those who have been abandoned there overnight. The compound is divided into separate rooms for different illnesses
and each room contains neat rows of dying people lying on
iron beds. It is a very unnerving sight.

The sisters themselves follow a rigorous routine. Their day
starts at 5am and follows a set rhythm: practical care for
those they are looking after, personal prayer, times of rest and
eating, and corporate prayer with the other sisters. Through
this rhythm they are given the strength they need to face the
demands of each day.

Few of us are called to lead the life that these sisters led.
Yet all of us in different ways are called to be activists for the
kingdom of God. Just consider these well-known words from
Isaiah 58:

'Is not this the kind of fasting I have chosen:
to loose the chains of injustice
    and untie the cords of the yoke,
to set the oppressed free
    and break every yoke?

> Is it not to share your food with the hungry
> > to provide the poor wanderer with shelter –
> when you see the naked, to clothe them,
> > and not to turn away from your own flesh and blood? ...
> If you do away with the yoke of oppression,
> > with the pointing finger and malicious talk,
> and if you spend yourselves on behalf of the hungry
> > and satisfy the needs of the oppressed,
> then your light will rise in the darkness,
> > and your night will become like the noonday.'
> (Is. 58:6–7, 9b–10)

This passage is found in the final part of Isaiah, which describes what Alec Motyer calls 'the characteristics of a waiting people'; a people seeking to live an obedient life while waiting for the Lord.[1] The previous verses (2–5) describe the kind of fasting that God does not want. It is fasting that tries to manipulate a response from God (compare 1 Kgs. 18:16–29) and, for whatever reasons, leads only to exploitation and fights. Instead of using the time freed up by fasting for meaningless rituals (verse 5), the time should be spent working towards a just society (verse 6), taking care of the individual needs of both strangers and family members (verse 7) and ensuring that personal behaviour is in line with such a social response (verses 9–10).[2]

These are hardly passive words; it is not possible to do these things without becoming actively involved in what is going on in the world around us. This book is aimed at helping those who want to spend themselves on behalf of the hungry and satisfy the needs of the oppressed. We can be activists in any number of ways: through writing letters, using our money wisely, looking at the impact our lifestyle has on the Earth, or marching through our streets. Whatever we do, we do it in order to see God's righteousness and justice extended from heaven, God's realm, into our world now.

So let us look further at why we should be activists.

First, we are to be activists because *activism is rooted right in the heart and character of God himself,* as Father, Son and Holy Spirit. The Bible story tells of a trinitarian God who is actively involved with his people, working out his plans for the salvation of the whole world. One of the best expressions of the character of God is in Psalm 146:

> He upholds the cause of the oppressed
>   and gives food to the hungry.
> The LORD sets prisoners free,
>   the LORD gives sight to the blind,
> the LORD lifts up those who are bowed down,
>   the LORD loves the righteous.
> The LORD watches over the alien
>   and sustains the fatherless and the widow,
>   but he frustrates the ways of the wicked.
> (Ps. 46:7–9)

God's plans for salvation find their fulfilment in the active nature of Jesus, the Son, who came down to this earth as a human being in order to restore and reconcile the world to God.[3] The incarnation is the ultimate expression of God's compassion as he enters into his creation, taking on our suffering. Jesus' life continues this demonstration of his compassion for those around him, and his twin emphasis on the poor and on proclaiming the good news is best captured in what many would see as his manifesto:

> The Spirit of the Lord is on me,
>   because he has anointed me
>   to preach good news to the poor.

He has sent me to proclaim freedom for the prisoners
and recovery of sight for the blind,
to release the oppressed,
to proclaim the year of the Lord's favour.
(Luke 4:18–19)

Jesus came in order that people 'may have life, and have it
to the full' (John 10:10), and he accomplished this by his life,
death and resurrection.[4]

Secondly, we are to be activists because *activism is the call
that God has placed on us*. Those earlier words from Isaiah 58
make that clear, and so does Micah 6:8:

He has showed you, O people, what is good.
And what does the Lord require of you?
To act justly and to love mercy
and to walk humbly with your God.

So does Proverbs 29:7:

The righteous care about justice for the poor,
but the wicked have no such concern.

Indeed, the whole way in which the nation of Israel was
established demonstrated that God's people were to be
different from those around them. One of the main ways in
which they were to be different was through their treatment
of other people and the land that God had created. So they
were to look after those who were vulnerable and unable to
look after themselves (see e.g. Deut. 10:18–19; Exod. 22:22),
and laws were put in place to prevent huge inequalities
appearing (e.g. the laws against moving boundary stones,
Deut. 19:14; 27:17). The best-known of these laws are the
Jubilee laws of Leviticus 25. These recognized the reality that

differences in material status would appear, but sought to ensure that limits were put on that. While a person could gain extra land and reap the benefits of the income it brought, that land was eventually to be returned to the original owner at the time of the Jubilee.[5] The foundation for all these laws was the experience of Israel's suffering in Egypt and her covenant relationship with a God who has an active love for justice (e.g. Lev. 25:39–43).

Jesus' parable of the Good Samaritan in Luke 10 similarly urges us to be actively involved with those around us. The question asked by the expert in the law is effectively, 'Who is my neighbour, whom I should love as myself?' Jesus turns the answer round so that the neighbour is the one doing the active caring (rather than the one who needs to be cared for, as is often presumed), and tells the 'expert': 'Go, then, and *be* that neighbour yourself.' There is no excuse allowed for knowing of someone's distress and doing nothing about it. James emphasizes this too when he stresses that the mark of a religion that is acceptable to God is that we 'look after orphans and widows in their distress and ... keep [ourselves] from being polluted by the world' (Jas. 1:27).

Just as the Israelites' experience of redemption was the foundation for their care of the poor, so it is Jesus' death for us that gives us the ultimate reason for our calling to be activists on behalf of those who are in need:

> This is how we know what love is: Jesus Christ laid down his life for us. And we ought to lay down our lives for one another. If anyone of you has material possessions and sees a brother or sister in need but has no pity on them, how can the love of God be in you? Dear children, let us not love with words or tongue but with actions and in truth.
>
> (1 John 3:16–18)

Thirdly, we are to be activists because *people have been made in the image of God* (Gen. 1:26–27). The fact that this phrase has been debated all through church history warns us against locating its meaning too narrowly and seeing it as referring exclusively to, for example, our rationality or our sense of morality. The phrase has many dimensions (more of which we shall see in 'C is for Creation'). One important dimension is our creation as relational beings and particularly our ability to have an intimate relationship with God – one of the key things that distinguishes us from the rest of creation. This is wonderfully captured by Augustine, who famously prayed, 'You have made us for yourself, and our hearts are restless until they find their rest in you.' There is a spiritual dimension within all of us that is an integral part of our being and of what it means to be human.

This is important in understanding why we should be activists in our world today. It is highlighted by the covenant that God made with Noah, which sees our creation in the image of God as the reason we are accountable for one another (Gen. 9:5–6). So our relationship with God is extended to our relationship with one another. A person who is viewed as just a physical being, devoid of all spiritual orientation, is, in essence, dehumanized. When we lose our true humanity, we must search for it elsewhere; hence the rampant rise of materialism. When we lose our true humanity, we lose our basis for compassion and concern, and this is what leads to the terrible injustices that happen in our world.

Fourthly, we should be activists because of *the state of our world*. Today, as you read this, 24,000 people will die of hunger and 6,000 children will die of diarrhoea. There are 149 million malnourished children in developing countries; 1,200 million people living on less than $1 a day; 100 million children without access to basic education; 1.1 million African children under fifteen living with HIV, and 1,100 million people without access to safe drinking water.[6] Moving closer to home, in the UK there are 13 million people living on a low income and 85,000 households in temporary accommodation.[7] If we believe that each one of these people has been made in the image of God, how can we not be active in working to see change?

Finally, we are to be activists because of *our hope for the future*. The above statistics make for depressing reading and lead to a sombre recognition that, because of the effects of the fall, the world is not as it should be and we shall never sort everything out in the present. The good news of Jesus is that we can look forward to a very different future, one that we begin to experience now through his life, death and resurrection, but that will be brought in fully when he comes again (Eph. 1:13–14).

The final chapters of Revelation give us a picture of that future, when there will be 'no more death or mourning or crying or pain' (21:4) and when the river of the water of life will flow and the tree of life will bear fruit (22:1–2). It is this future hope that gives us our motivation for how we live today, in the same way that Paul's teaching on the future always led him straight into encouraging us to live a godly life in the present (e.g. 1 Cor. 15; 1 Thess. 4:13 – 5:11). In the frequently quoted words of Jürgen Moltmann, 'from first to last, and not merely in the epilogue, Christianity is eschatology, is hope, forward looking and forward moving, and therefore also revolutionizing and transforming the present'.[8]

As we live in the tension between the 'now' that Jesus' first coming has brought and the 'not yet' that will be realized with his second coming, we are to demonstrate an active attitude of 'expectancy and anticipation'.[9] Our role is to be living examples of the future, anticipating now what we know the future holds. In that way,

21

Because of the victory Jesus has already achieved by his resurrection, his followers are never driven to despair even when faced with the most appalling social conditions. They are called rather to an active participation in that new movement in history which takes God's intentions and purposes for mankind as their own. However limited or imperfect his impact may be, a Christian 'knows that every stand he takes for social righteousness and every effort he makes towards social renewal and justice and tolerance is not lost'.[10]

What sort of activists, then, should we be?

First, as the Sisters of Charity so beautifully demonstrate, we should be *prayerful* activists. Prayer connects us with the people and situations around the world for whom or for which we are praying. It reminds us of our motivation: to see the kingdom of God manifest in our world. It reminds us that there is a strong spiritual dimension to all that we do. Above all, prayer reminds us that we cannot do everything by ourselves or in our own power. Ultimately we depend on God to bring his redeeming power to bear in the situations in which we work. Prayer also causes us to stop and take time for reflection. Activists are not action-junkies and taking time to rest is a thoroughly biblical thing to do.[11]

Secondly, we should be *knowledgeable* activists. The problems that face our world are immensely complicated and it does not do to be simplistic or naïve. Books, magazines, websites, TV and radio programmes are all good places to look for information. One of the best things we can do is join an organization that can point us to the resources that will help us the most.

Thirdly, we should be *gracious* activists. It can be all too easy, once we start to understand why we should be activists, to become self-righteous and moralistic, preaching to everyone else about where *their* lifestyle is wrong. Jesus made it clear that we must focus on our own failures first (Matt. 7:3–5). It may take all our lives to remove the plank in our own eyes before we are able to remove the speck from someone else's!

Being activists is what this book is about. The following chapters are aimed at giving us knowledge and a way forward along this route.

Action points

- Find out about the organizations listed below. Check out their websites and begin to build up your knowledge on some of the issues we shall be looking at in further chapters.

- As you do so, ask God to give you vision and fill you with Jesus' compassion.

Good contacts

Cred: PO Box 58, Chichester, West Sussex, PO19 8UD; 01243 783968; <www.cred.org.uk>
Speak: The Shop, 487 Liverpool Road, London, N7 8PG; 0207609 1744; <www.speak.org.uk>
Tearfund: 100 Church Road, Teddington, Middlesex, TW11 8QE; 0845 355 8355; <www.tearfund.org>
World Development Movement: 25 Beehive Place, London, SW9 7QR; 0207737 6215; <www.wdm.org.uk>

Good books

G. Haugen, *Good News About Injustice*
M. Northcott, *Life After Debt: Christianity and Global Justice*
R. Sider, *Rich Christians in an Age of Hunger*

B is for Bananas

My daughter loves bananas, and her grandma often tells her that one day she will end up looking like one. Bananas have become one of the basic foods that we all eat today: so basic that the banana is the world's most popular fruit, worth £5 billion a year, and in the UK 95% of households buy them. We eat more bananas than we do apples; they are the most valuable food product in supermarkets, outsold only by petrol and lottery tickets.[1]

Yet my parents' generation almost never ate them. Do we ever stop to think what has taken place in order for bananas to be such an ordinary part of our lives, rather than an exotic fruit that we rarely see? As commonplace as they may seem, bananas are the perfect way to introduce us to the big, complex game that is global trade.[2]

This is the story of the Banana War. Traditionally, Britain and the rest of the European Union have bought their bananas from their former colonies, particularly the Windward Islands in the Caribbean. Britain invested in the original plantations, and Geest, the company that buys and sells most of the bananas, is a British company. The Lomé Convention in 1975 formalized the EU's commitment to continue to import bananas from the Windward Islands. This commitment was crucial, since the Windward Islands are almost totally reliant on their banana industry and are able to charge a better price for their bananas than producers elsewhere.

Seventy per cent of the bananas involved in international

trade, however, are controlled by the big three American companies: Chiquita, Dole and Del Monte.[3] Not liking the EU protectionist policy on bananas, America complained to the World Trade Organization (WTO), which ruled in favour of the USA. When the EU refused to back down, the US struck back and imposed import tariffs, in the end worth $191.4 million, on EU exports (hitting companies such as Arran Aromatics in Scotland, which found 40% of its turnover affected). It might come as no surprise that the American complaint to the WTO came just days after Chiquita donated $500,000 to the Democratic Party, and that the tariffs were enforced by the Republican-controlled Congress after Chiquita donated $350,000 to them.

Today, the overwhelming majority of the bananas that we consume are produced in appalling circumstances. There are two main issues here. First, the plantation workers live in poverty. In Ecuador, for example, the workers are paid just $1 a day, and some independent producers get only 3p per pound (450 g), which does not even cover costs. On average, the producer gets only 5% of the price of a banana; as with many other commodities exported to the North, 90% of the price stays in the North and is never seen by the producer.

Secondly, vast quantities of chemicals are used to treat the bananas during their production. Plantations in Central America apply 30 kg of active ingredients per hectare per year; this is more than ten times the average for intensive farming in industrialized countries. In Costa Rica, three-quarters of banana workers suffer from skin lesions and 20% of the male workers became sterile due to handling pesticides, while entire communities suffer from indiscriminate aerial crop-spraying.

The impact on the environment need hardly be stated, let alone the fact that massive deforestation has taken place to provide the land for the plantations. The effect that all these chemicals have on those of us who eat them is something we shall consider in a later chapter. It is interesting to note, however, the response of a banana worker on a Chiquita plantation in Guatemala, on being asked if he ever ate the bananas he produced: 'Good Lord, no! ... People in places like this don't eat the fruit they cut. I guess we know better.'

Although we are focusing on bananas, it is no surprise to learn that many other foods are also produced and traded in ways that do great damage to the producers. Chocolate is made from cocoa, which is grown and harvested on many plantations that are worked on by modern-day slaves. In West Africa, forest land has been cleared to be planted with cocoa trees and is tended by boys and young men who come from poor neighbouring countries looking for work. They work in awful situations. Many are unable to escape and are brutally beaten if caught trying to do so. It is thought that 90% of the plantations in the Ivory Coast use slaves, and up to 40% of the chocolate that we eat may be contaminated with slavery.[4]

The price of drinking coffee is going up, yet the price paid for raw coffee beans has fallen to its lowest level since the 1930s and only looks set to get worse. This has hit coffee producers hard and many are now living in extreme poverty. Nine-tenths of the price that we pay for instant coffee goes to the companies that ship, roast and sell the product and, in some cases, just one fiftieth reaches the producers. It may come as no surprise, therefore, that the large coffee-roasting houses such as Sara Lee and Nestlé have gained massive profits. Nestlé, for example, saw a rise in profits of 20% in 2001.[5]

This list could be continued to include other foodstuffs – such as tea, sugar and rice – and also goods such as clothes, electronic goods and children's toys. It is a harsh reality that we are able to buy the things we do, at the price we enjoy, because those who are making or producing them are not being paid a proper wage by the large companies that own them.

But are there alternatives, and is there anything that we can do about it?

The answer is 'yes' to both questions. There are three routes open to us. The first is *Fair trade*. Fair trade (FT) schemes work directly with cooperatives, cutting out the middlemen. They guarantee a fixed minimum price, however low world prices may fall, and, if prices rise above this level, some schemes (such as Cafédirect) pay an extra 10% social premium. They often help beyond just making the payments, with business development programmes and other advice. FT schemes are incredibly beneficial to the producers. For example, despite the recent coffee crisis, those registered with the official FT scheme were able to escape its worse effects and still invest in essentials such as healthcare and education.

Many FT products are now readily available in our shops and are doing extremely well, showing a year-on-year average increase of 50%, with the range expanding constantly.[6] Coffee, tea and chocolate can be bought in supermarkets, and FT bananas are now on the shelves of Asda, the Co-op, Tesco, Safeway, Sainsbury's and Waitrose.[7] Many city centres have FT shops and Traidcraft is one example of the FT mail-order possibilities.

FT succeeds when the whole supply chain can be controlled, and hence works best with foodstuffs and also with cotton clothing. FT is the ideal that must be striven for. The present reality, though, is that few companies can truthfully assert that they know how all their goods are produced, since a typical supply chain is vast. (Sainsbury's, for example, estimates that it takes the produce of a million farms around the globe.)[8]

With this in mind, the second alternative route available to us, where FT is not yet an option, is to push for *ethical trade.* Ethical trade is about ensuring that minimum international labour standards are met. These standards include freely chosen employment; freedom to form trade unions; safe and hygienic working conditions; no child labour; payment of living wages; no excessive working hours; minimum environmental damage and no discrimination.[9] For this to happen, companies need to be prepared to aim for longer-term solutions, improving supply chains through incremental changes. Most of the goods we buy will not carry a FT label, but we can still play our part in encouraging companies to operate more ethically by becoming more educated and informed about the products we are purchasing and asking questions of the companies whenever we want to buy from them.

The third route is *trade justice.* One of the main ways a country can be lifted out of its poverty is through increasing its exports to the richer countries. The rules for international trade, however, are governed by the commercial and financial interests of those richer countries and thus are shaped to their own advantage. These rules are enforced primarily through three institutions: the WTO, the International Monetary Fund and the World Bank.[10] Trade justice is about seeing a major overhaul happen to the current system so that the rules work *for* poor people rather than against them. This reform of the institutions would include measures like making poverty eradication a key objective, ensuring a truly democratic and transparent process and monitoring the activities of transnational corporations as well as of governments.[11] As citizens and consumers we can be using our voices to call for these changes to take place.[12]

With so many avenues open to us, we can begin playing our part in changing, for the good, the lives of the people who grow or make the things we buy. We have already seen how Jesus' parable of the Good Samaritan teaches us that we are to be neighbours to those whom others ignore, and this applies to those living next door and those on the other side of the world. Through taking the time and trouble to buy fairly traded products, and by getting involved in working for a fairer and more ethical trading system, we can take a step towards being that neighbour ourselves.

Action points

- Increase your awareness of the issues behind the products you buy. Take time to ask retailers where the product comes from and whether they have looked into the conditions of the producers. For more information on food and supermarkets, see 'F is for Food'.

- Whenever you can, make sure that the things you buy carry the fair-trade logo. This will often mean shopping somewhere other than the supermarket and being prepared to pay a higher price. If you find this hard to swallow, tell yourself that you are paying the price you should be paying anyway and are stopping others getting ripped off.

- Consider setting up a Traidcraft stall at your place of work or worship. That way, you and others can gain access to a greater number of fairly traded goods than the supermarkets provide.

- Find out more about the Trade Justice Movement and consider how you might get involved.

Good contacts

Ethical Consumer magazine (the *Which?* of the ethical world): Unit 21, 41 Old Birley Street, Manchester M15 5RF; 0161 229 2929; <www.ethicalconsumer.org>

Ethical Trading Initiative: 2nd Floor, Cromwell House,
14 Fulwood Place, London WC1V 6HZ;
<www.ethicaltrade.org>
The Fairtrade Foundation: Suite 204, 16 Baldwin's Gardens,
London EC1N 7RJ; <www.fairtrade.org.uk>
Labour Behind the Label (for information on clothes and
toys): 38 Exchange Street, Norwich NR2 1AX; 01603
610993; <lbl@gn.apc.org>
Traidcraft: Kingsway, Gateshead, Tyne and Wear NE11 0NE;
0191 491 0591; <www.traidcraft.co.uk>

C is for Creation

I am pleased that C comes so near the beginning of the
alphabet and that creation can be one of the first things we
consider, because it is such a vitally important subject.
Certainly, those outside the church seem to recognize this:
governments and businesses are keen to show their environmental credentials and any conference worth its salt will
feature the environment on its agenda somewhere. Yet the
sad fact is that, somehow, the church does not view it as such
a priority and that is strange because, while others may talk
about the environment, we are talking about *creation*.

Christians believe in a trinitarian God – Father, Son and
Holy Spirit – who has made the universe and the world that
we live in (regardless of theories of evolution) and who has

declared that it is 'very good' (Gen. 1:31). Some theologies have taught too much of a separation between body and spirit, earth and heaven, natural and spiritual; exalting the latter and denigrating the former so that nature/creation is thought to be inferior to the supernatural realm. In contrast to this, the world carries within it the intrinsic value of something that God has made and finds pleasure in – and note that God pronounced creation 'good' before humanity was created. Because he has made it, it belongs to him, first and foremost, and to humanity only secondly (Ps. 24:1). While we are appointed to govern on his behalf (Gen. 1:26–30), it is only through his continual influence that the Earth is sustained. One of the key biblical principles arising out of this is that the right of all to use the Earth's resources comes before anyone's right to ownership.[1] The Earth, then, has been given to us not as something that God no longer cares about, but as a gift that we are to treasure and look after.

In the Old Testament the idea of dominion is used of the Hebrew kings and embodies within it the idea of 'servant kingship', reflecting God's own kingly rule within creation, which is undoubtedly a caring and providing one rather than one of domination.[2] Genesis 1:26–28, however, has caused problems in the church through a misunderstanding of the words 'dominion' and 'subdue' and hence a misunderstanding of the account of creation as a whole. This has led some to an anthropocentric view of creation that holds that everything revolves around humanity and was made for our benefit.[3] It is certainly true that there is a distinction between human beings and the rest of creation; we are the only ones to have been made 'in the image of God' and to have been set apart to have dominion over the rest of creation. This can be seen in Adam's naming the animals – a significant act in the Bible (and it is interesting to note that the Muslim account of creation has God, not Adam, giving the animals their names).

Because of this distinction between humanity and the rest of creation, the psalmist can describe humanity as being a little lower than the heavenly beings (or God) and crowned with glory and splendour, and as having the rest of God's creation 'under their feet' (Ps. 8:5–6).

That distinction between humanity and the rest of creation, though, needs to be held in tension with the reality that we are also a part of creation and not superior to it. It is an inescapable fact that we are part of the same ecosystems and structures that form the rest of creation. In fact, as Professor C. J. H. Wright states, the opening chapters of Genesis 'do not immediately emphasize human uniqueness. On the contrary, it seems that at point after point we have more in common with the rest of the animate creation than in distinction from it.'[4] We might even question the popular interpretation that sees humanity as the climax of creation, since a less human-centred approach would see the real consummation and goal of creation as God's rest on day seven, which reminds us that all creation exists for God, to worship him, rather than for humanity.[5]

Of immense significance in the creation narrative is the description of humanity (and humanity alone) as being made 'in God's image'. We began to explore what this phrase means in 'A is for Activists'. One meaning that the author of Genesis particularly highlights is to do with the role that we are given regarding the rest of creation. Indeed, Professor Wright makes the point that the grammar used in Genesis 1:26–28 indicates that this is one of the main reasons why humanity is so made: 'because God intended this last-created species, the human species, to exercise dominion over the rest of his creatures, for that reason God expressly and purposefully creates this species alone in his own image'. The sense of the verses could then be read as, 'Let us make human beings in our own image and likeness, *so that* they may exercise dominion over the rest of creation'.[6]

'The image of God' carries the idea of being God's representative on earth in the same way that physical images of a king would be set up throughout his territory to signal his lordship. By being made in his image, God has given us delegated authority over his creation. It should go without saying that we exercise that authority in a way that reflects his character, not through brutality and carelessness, but with love and compassion and service.

Our representation of the image of God, however, has been marred by the fall because humanity turned away from God and chose to go their own way. The fall broke humanity's relationship with God, with other humans and with the rest of creation, which would now carry within itself the curse of God as well as his blessing. The rest of the Bible tells the story of the unfolding plan of God for salvation. Israel is called to be his people and model his purposes for servant kingship, and there is a particular relationship with the land that acts as a spiritual barometer of her obedience.[7]

Our relationship with the rest of creation finds its centre in the coming of Jesus to live on earth as a human being, to die and to be raised to life again. God's plan finds its fulfilment in Jesus, who affirms creation by choosing to become a part of that creation and, by dying and being raised to life again, brings potential healing to every broken relationship.[8] It is crucial to understand that God's intention for salvation involves the whole of creation, not just humanity alone (see also Col. 1:15–20).

Revelation 4 is a stunning vision of the whole of creation, including human beings, worshipping the Lord God Almighty. This is the end for which we have been made; to worship God completely and to enable the rest of creation to be made perfect in order to praise its Creator. This is a great privilege, but also an awesome responsibility. As Colin Gunton says, 'we human creatures are the centre of the world's problems, and

33

only by our redirection will the whole creation be set free'.[9] Here, therefore, we see that, if evangelism and social transformation are to be truly reflecting God's mission, we must also be involved in ecological care.[10]

The Bible ends with a wonderful picture of the new heaven and the new earth (Rev. 21 – 22). This picture in Revelation describes how the world that God has made as the new Jerusalem comes down from heaven – we do not 'go up there'. All things are made new in Jesus, involving all of creation as the tree of life bears its fruit for all humanity to enjoy and the curse of the fall is finally ended. In a manner similar to our own resurrected bodies, there is both discontinuity (seen in 2 Pet. 3:3–16) and continuity (seen in Rom. 8:18–30) between the present and the new heaven and earth.[11] The emphasis of the word 'new' is on transformation rather than destruction, indicating 'newness in terms of quality rather than of something new that has never been in existence'.[12] In this way, we understand 'the new creation itself not as a replacement for the present world but as the eschatological future of this world'.[13]

This spurs us on to action. In 'A is for Activists' we saw how our future hope gives us the motivation for how we live today, in active expectancy and anticipation. Just as the incentive for our lives is to be seeing God's kingdom brought into this world now, so too, no less, with the rest of creation: it is our future hope that inspires us to work for its present, albeit partial, realization.

What does that mean for us?

First, we need to be learning about the major threats to God's creation. These are issues such as climate change, deforestation, the loss of species and biodiversity, consumer waste and pollution. We shall be exploring all of these things further in later chapters.

Secondly, we can then begin to consider what we can do in

34

our own lives to start making a difference. When looking at such huge problems it can be helpful to see ourselves standing within concentric circles, each circle representing a wider area for involvement. These areas are: ourselves, our church, our local community, our country, our world.

So, for example, we can change some of the everyday things we do, perhaps increasing what we recycle or reducing our car usage. In our churches, maybe we could consider carrying out an environmental audit (Christian Ecology Link, below, can help) or, again, simply encourage people to walk or cycle to church. In our local communities there may be a conservation organization or Local Agenda 21 programme we could join. Perhaps we could encourage our local authorities to improve recycling facilities. When we move on to our country and world we begin to enter the area of campaigning and letter-writing. Here it is useful to belong to a national or international organization that will help us in this. Again, we shall look more closely at a lot of these things in later chapters.

What we have to remember is that we cannot do everything. But that is no reason to do nothing! While each little action we take *is* only a drop in the ocean, those drops will make a difference. Not only is this our responsibility; it is a part of the essence of being people created by God that we care for the rest of what he has created.

Action points

- Increase your awareness and understanding of the created world in which you live. Stop to smell a flower, notice a particular colour, watch a bird fly, follow the seasons in your garden ...

- Find out about the organizations listed below and, if financially able, join the one that you think will help you the most.

35

Good contacts
A Rocha: 3 Hooper Street, Cambridge, CB1 2NZ; 01387
710286; <www.arocha.org>
Christian Ecology Link: 20 Carlton Road, Harrogate
HG2 8DD; 01423 871616; <www.Christian-ecology.org.uk>
Friends of the Earth: 26–28 Underwood Street, London
N1 7RQ; 020 7490 1555; <www.foe.co.uk>

Good books
R. J. Berry (ed.), *The Care of Creation*
K. Gnanakan, *God's World: A Theology of the Environment*
G. Prance, *The Earth Under Threat*

D is for Driving [1]

We've all seen the advertisements on the TV: just you, in your
car, driving along an empty road. To drive a car is the stuff
that life is made of. You are in control; you have the money
and the look; you have the power to make your life whatever
you want it to be. In a world of confusion and instability, your
car is the one thing you can rely on: a safe haven from life's
storms. Your car is, indeed, a car to be proud of.

There is no doubt that the car has brought many benefits.
It is convenient to hop into the car and nip to the shops. In
winter it is more comfortable and, in our busy lives, driving
saves so much time. It increases our employment options,

allowing us to take a job some distance away, and helps us keep in touch with our scattered family and friends.

It is amazing to think how, over the course of just a few decades, our lifestyles have become so dependent on the car. There are 480 million cars in the world and nearly 29 million new cars are made each year: car traffic is expected to increase by 22% by 2010. Of those 480 million, 90% are owned by the sixteen wealthiest countries (one fifth of the world's population). In the UK we use the car for more and more of our shorter journeys. Twenty-five per cent of car trips are under two miles and 61% are under five miles.

As we look at these statistics, it does not take much to pierce through the façade of the car ads and to see that, whatever the benefits, our car-dependent culture is also bringing great costs. The first cost is to ourselves. The emissions from a car consist of carbon monoxide, carbon dioxide, lead, nitrogen dioxide, benzene, hydrocarbons and particulates. None of these is good for our health! Indeed, benzene is a known cancer-causing chemical, and it is no coincidence that the number of asthma cases has doubled in the UK in the last fifteen years. Road traffic is the fastest-growing source of air pollution and constitutes 70% of carbon monoxide emissions. Interestingly, tests show that, in heavy traffic, pollution levels are higher inside a car than outside. In contrast to the health problems caused by driving, a regular adult cyclist shows the fitness level of a person ten years younger than a non-cyclist of the same age.[2]

The problem is even worse in other parts of the world. *The Times of India* states that breathing the air in Mumbai (formerly Bombay) and Delhi is the equivalent of smoking twenty cigarettes a day. In Mexico, the situation is so serious that everybody is banned from driving their cars one day a week, each car being identified by a number on the number plate.

As well as our health, the increase in car usage has had a dramatic impact on our communities. Parents are afraid to let their children walk to school or play outside because of the traffic. This is understandable when you consider that the most common cause of death for children under fifteen is a road accident. A transport survey in West Sussex found that 70% of children lived within half a mile of their school, but 45% were regularly driven to school. Of those 45%, 30% of parents said they would walk or cycle if road safety improvements were made.[3]

It is interesting, too, that car ownership is one of the main indicators of the increasing inequality that is found in the UK. About a third of households do not have a car, yet town planning and design favours those with cars, with its emphasis on out-of-town shopping centres. People without cars are forced to shop in the smaller, local shops where goods are more expensive. We have seen already how the Old Testament laws such as the Jubilee sought to limit the inequalities that existed between people. For Christians, the improvement of access for all is an issue of equality and justice and we should seize any opportunity to campaign for better-quality public transport and for policies that keep our town centres vibrant.

The second cost is to the environment. We shall look at climate change later, but it is relevant to note here that cars produce a fifth of the UK's carbon dioxide emissions and it is expected that fuel consumption from private-car owners will increase globally by up to 130% in twenty-five years.

The effect that road-building has on the countryside was highlighted dramatically by the protests around the building of the M3 through the wetland meadows and chalk grasslands of Twyford Down, and the building of the Newbury Bypass through the precious heathland of Snelsmore Common. Road-building threatens priceless wildlife sites and kills millions of animals. Our petrol comes from the oil that is imported into Britain on sea tankers. There have been several well-publicized and horrific oil disasters, not least that of the *Sea Empress*, which ran aground off Wales in 1996 and spilled 70,000 tonnes of crude oil, ruining the local fishing industry and destroying countless numbers of wildlife and seabirds.

Does it have to be like this? The answer, of course, is no, and there are some inspiring examples of places where people live differently. There is a European network of 'car-free cities' that work on the idea that quality of life is greatly improved by not having to provide for cars. Such places are not absolutely car-less, but operate car-sharing schemes. These schemes have reduced the members' mileage by 50% and increased their use of public transport. In Bremen, for example, each shared car is thought to have replaced five private cars. *Tomorrow's World* sums up the advantages of these places as being 'less noise, pollution, energy use and danger, and more green space, money (the average car costs £3,117 a year to run), local trade and freedom for children'.[4]

But what about the majority of us who cannot live in such places? Is there anything we can do to make a difference?

The obvious answer, of course, is that we must all reduce our dependency on our cars and cut down the amount of times that we use them. *There is no other way round it*; we have to start walking or cycling for those shorter journeys and using public transport for the longer ones. It is an amazing fact that there are an estimated 22 million bikes in the UK, with only 5 million regularly being used. Cycling accounts for only 2% of journeys, whereas, in the Netherlands, it accounts for 27%. If we could raise our figure to 18% we would save 10 million tonnes of carbon dioxide.[5] A positive example is the organization Pedals, which was set up to encourage more people to use bikes and to campaign for safer and more attractive cycling conditions in the

Nottingham area. It has helped Nottingham to develop one of the country's largest networks of urban cycle routes.

A lot of this is about changing our attitudes. We have got so used to driving short distances that the thought of walking or cycling is not a pleasant one; it is so much more *convenient* to drive. We are cocooned in a culture that sees inconvenience as one of the greatest evils, to be avoided at all costs, and so we confuse what we perceive to be a need with what actually is just a nuisance: 'It takes more trouble to cycle or walk, therefore I need to drive.' My mum used to cycle eight miles to school and back every day, even in the rain or the snow. That was nothing amazing – it was just what you did. I sometimes think of that if I am feeling that I would rather drive the 1.5 miles to the leisure centre.

What I have found is that what begins as a discipline ends up becoming a pleasure. I now complain if it is pouring with rain and I drive somewhere with my daughter rather than cycle! I now love to walk or cycle. I love the fact that I am outside; that I am not damaging God's creation in any way. I love the fact that I am getting some exercise; that I am more aware of what the seasons are doing; that I can appreciate the flowers in people's gardens and the birds in the hedges; that I can say hello to people from my neighbourhood and stop for a chat. I love the fact that my daughter is growing up not under the impression that all journeys have to be made in a car.

Realistically, though, many of us will want to own and use a car and there are still many things we can do here to make a difference. Always look for ways to car-share: if you know of someone else going to the same place as you, phone them up and offer them a lift. When driving, keep your speed down. Driving at 50 mph uses 25% less fuel than driving at 70. I have had to do this gradually. I used to drive regularly at 80 mph (and felt virtuous for keeping my speed down to that!). When I began learning about the environmental costs, I decided to slow down. To jump from 80 mph to 60 is painfully frustrating, so I weaned myself off five miles at a time: driving at 75 mph until that felt normal, then down to 70 and so on until now I leave home a bit early and drive at 60, even on long journeys. Yes, it is aggravatingly slow, but you do get used to it and the benefits to the environment and to your purse are worth it! Alongside that, braking and accelerating gently reduces your fuel consumption, whereas using air conditioning increases it.

Keeping your car in good condition improves efficiency. If your car was built before 1993, fit a catalytic converter. Do remember, though, that these only kick in after two miles. Look into having an emissions-saving device fitted. These can reduce emissions by 40% and save at least 10% on fuel costs.[6] Next time you buy a car, choose one that is highly efficient or buy a hybrid car (running on both petrol and electricity). These produce 75% less pollution than ultra-low-emission vehicles.

Finally, we must make sure that we do not fall into the trap of thinking that, if we are being more environmentally sensitive with our cars, it is OK to drive them more! Every time a car is started up, the world God made is damaged in some way. Sadly, every little trip to the supermarket contributes to global warming. As we saw in the previous chapter, the way we treat our world is a fundamental part of what it means to be a Christian. Someone once said to me that to be a disciple of Jesus and knowingly to harm his creation is a contradiction in terms. That is a sobering thought in relation to the amount we drive. So let's drive in a way that is as least damaging as possible, and, whenever we can, leave that car at home!

Action points
- Stop using your car for all short distances (and be prepared to lengthen your idea of a short distance).

- If you have a bicycle, get it serviced so that is in good condition.

- Begin to drive more slowly.

- Fit an emissions-reducing device to your car.

Good contacts
Environmental Transport Association: 10 Church Street, Weybridge, Surrey KT13 8RS; 01932 828882; <info@eta.co.uk>
Sustrans: 35 King Street, Bristol BS1 4DZ; 0117 929 0888; <info@sustrans.org.uk>

E is for Energy

The first thing I did this morning was wake up and have a shower. The water was hot and the house warm, due to our gas central heating. I then got up Mali, our daughter, changed her nappy (which will need to be washed later) and gave her some milk, warmed in the microwave. I sat in bed and watched the news on TV and then we had breakfast: coffee made with water boiled in the kettle and cereal with milk kept cool in the fridge. This morning we went to our playgroup, which had a bouncy castle kept buoyant by an air pump. After lunch (toast made in the toaster), Mali is now sleeping and I am sitting here, writing on my computer.

Nearly all of those things required energy in the form of gas, petrol or electricity. I have done nothing out of the ordinary, but already I have used a good amount of energy. Even the water I am drinking has been through an energy-intensive process to rid it of, among other things, the chemicals put in it by industry and agriculture and from the cleaning products we use. The society we have created is totally dependent on using large amounts of energy in order to survive.

Nearly three-quarters of the energy that is used globally comes from fossil fuels (oil, coal and gas) and the rest is from nuclear, hydro and biomass. In the UK, nearly 90% of energy is from fossil fuels. The problems associated with them, however, are colossal.

At the forefront is climate change. This is caused by the releasing of harmful gases into the atmosphere (predominantly carbon dioxide) when fossil fuels are burned. These greenhouse gases trap the sun's heat in the atmosphere, leading to global warming, which results in the climate changing. This is having a devastating affect on our world with floods, droughts, storms and heatwaves trebling over the last thirty years, wreaking havoc the world over. In 1998, 26 million people were made homeless through flooding in Bangladesh. As temperatures rise and glaciers melt, sea levels are rising around the world, threatening low-lying coastal areas. The Maldives, for example, are likely to disappear altogether. At the other extreme, it is thought that, by 2050, over two billion people could face a water shortage.[1]

Alongside this, but forgotten under the urgency of climate change, is acid rain. This is caused by the mixing of water in the atmosphere with nitrogen and sulphur oxides, which then form sulphuric acid and nitric acid. These are still causing damage to lakes and forests around Europe.

43

Another very real problem is that of the depletion of the natural resources that we are using. While the *Limits to Growth* theory, which caused a public debate in 1972 through its doomsday predictions, may have been discredited, it is still a fact that we are using our resources at an unsustainable rate. For example, it is estimated that the amount of oil used globally in a year takes one million years to be formed.[2]

Oil is the key to all of this as it is essential to agriculture, petrochemicals and the production of the petrol and electricity that we use. Its extraction causes environmental degradation, and this only looks set to worsen as new reserves become harder to find and are opened in such fragile and beautiful places as Alaska, officially a National Wildlife Refuge.

Because of its central place in the global economy, and because we cannot survive without it, oil ('black gold') is a major factor in world politics. The first Gulf War was waged mainly because of the West's need to access Kuwait's oil.[3] A highly publicized case is Nigeria, where Shell and other companies are involved in oil extraction in Ogoniland. Protests from the Ogoni people that their land has been ruined and their livelihoods destroyed have been met with violence from the Nigerian Government. Since 1993, the Nigerian Internal Security forces have killed over a thousand Ogonis.[4] Oil now accounts for 80% of the country's GDP and 90% of Government revenues, yet the industry employs only 2% of all Nigerians and deep corruption means that the nation as a whole does not feel the benefit of the oil money. Alongside all of this is the Global Climate Coalition, formed by the fossil fuel companies to protect their profits and to lobby against any action taken to prevent further climate change. Esso has been at the forefront of this.[5]

It hardly needs to be stated that this way of operating runs strongly against God's intention for his creation. Two further points, particularly, can be made.

The first is to underline that our environmental crisis is, at its heart, a spiritual issue, linked with humanity's sin. Jon Sobrino has said that 'the question of the poor ... is fundamentally the question of God, and of what kind of God we worship'.[6] The same may be said of our regard for what God has created. Idolatry is central to our world, in which the false gods of wealth, power and security are worshipped in the place of the one true God.[7] The environmental problems associated with our current use of energy can be attributed to human greed and selfishness; to our consumer society, which expects an ever-increasing standard of living, and to the unrestricted growth of the rich nations. The average person in the UK uses 35 times as much energy as the average person in India.[8] This link between the misuse of the land and human sin is clearly seen in the Old Testament prophets. Hosea 4:1b–3 provides a good example:

'There is no faithfulness, no love,
   no acknowledgment of God in the land ...
Because of this the land mourns,
   and all who live in it waste away;
the beasts of the field and the birds of the air
   and the fish of the sea are dying'.

This brings us to the second point: that of the spiritual nature of species extinction, which is occurring at a rate 98% higher than is natural. Romans 1:20 makes it clear that creation reveals the character of God.[9] The story of Noah is about God's saving and loving care for all living things; the purpose of including two of every living thing in the ark was 'to keep their various kinds alive throughout the earth' (Gen. 7:3). Looking at it from this perspective, then, John Stott is right to say that 'extinction is blasphemy'; and Metropolitan Archbishop Daniel of Moldova makes the sad point that 'extinction is a loss of our knowledge of God – erasing his fingerprints'.

Our use of energy reflects our inability to imagine living any other way, and it is clear that our societies must wean themselves off the dependency on fossil fuels. Some cite nuclear power as an alternative. Primarily, this is because it has low carbon dioxide emissions. Safety scares, the real cost of nuclear power (subsidized by £1 billion a year in the 1990s) and the lack of solution to the problem of nuclear waste, however, mean that its drawbacks heavily outweigh any carbon dioxide benefits.

The alternative has to come from renewable energy: using the wind, water, tides, waves, biomass and solar energy that could be so readily available to us all. At the moment, only 2.8% of electricity in the UK comes from a renewable source. For this to increase, the UK Government must be prepared to put the necessary investment into developing these services.

So what are the areas in which we can begin to play our part? First, since transport is the fastest-growing source of carbon dioxide emissions, everything that we looked at in our last chapter applies here too: reduce car usage.

Secondly, since 25% of the UK's carbon dioxide emissions comes from our houses, there are many things we can do around the home to reduce our energy usage. We can use low-energy light-bulbs (which use 80% less energy); fit a SAVA plug on to our fridges and freezers; insulate our homes effectively and wash our clothes on cooler temperatures with full loads. (While on the subject of washing, the production of 'disposable' nappies uses far more energy than the washing of washable ones.) We should turn all appliances off standby: the energy used to keep all our TVs on standby would power Basingstoke. Similarly, if everyone boiled just the amount of water that was needed in the kettle, instead of filling it up, enough energy would be saved to power the whole of the UK's

streetlights for the following night.[10] Perhaps most importantly, we can reduce the amount of energy we use for our
heating and hot water. Turning the thermostat down by just
1°C or using one hour less heating a day can save 10% on fuel
bills, and showering uses a quarter of the water of a bath.[11] As
we do these things we shall reduce our own energy bills,
demonstrating that self-interest and global stewardship can
go hand in hand.

Thirdly, we can actively promote the use of renewable
energy by switching to a 'green' electricity supplier (such as
unit[e] or Ecotricity) or going on to a 'green' tariff with our
existing supplier (ScottishPower, Powergen and Southern
Electricity are the best). For more information about this
contact the Energy Saving Trust or the National Energy
Foundation (see below). Some conservation organizations
(such as the RSPB) have their own schemes affiliated to
'green' suppliers, and by switching to these we can go 'green'
and support our chosen organization at the same time.

47

Finally, we can write to our MPs asking them to put
pressure on the Government to provide more support for
renewable energy and energy efficiency and also to create
policies that will reduce the UK's carbon dioxide emissions.

Action points
- Decide on five ways in which you will reduce the amount
  of energy you use around the home. When you are doing
  these five easily, choose another five. If you live with your
  family, try to include them by asking them to imagine
  ways of reducing energy.

- Buy your electricity from a green supplier.

- Find out about Friends of the Earth's Climate Change
  Campaign and write to your MP.

Good contacts
Centre for Alternative Technology: Machynlleth, Powys
SY20 9AZ; 01654 702 400; <www.cat.org>
Energy Saving Trust: 21 Dartmouth St, London SW1H 9BP;
0345 277200; <www.est.org.uk>
Friends of the Earth: see 'C is for Creation'
National Energy Foundation: Davy Avenue, Knowlhill,
Milton Keynes MK5 8NG; 01908 665555;
<www.greenenergy.org.uk>

F is for Food

I am obsessed with food. There are no two ways about it: food
is the subject that I will talk about most passionately and
about which I am becoming frighteningly puritanical! So
what has happened to cause this mania in me? I blame it all
on the innocent boxes of locally grown organic vegetables
that have been coming to our house every week for the last
few years.

To begin with I really disliked the scheme. The vegetables
were often dirty, needing a good soak and a scrub, taking up
time. I found the seasonal aspect of it frustrating and I
disliked the blemishes and imperfections that the vegetables
sometimes had on them.

Over the last few years, however, these vegetables have
taken me on a journey of discovery about the food we eat. I

now look at these things in a completely new light. These days I love the fact that my food comes with the soil still attached to it. It reminds me that my food does not come from a plastic bag, but from the ground. Scrubbing the soil off my carrots gives me some little contact with the earth that has produced it and reminds me of the labour that has gone into growing it.

I now love the fact that the vegetables come in seasons. Again, it brings me back into contact with nature, away from the bright lights and plastic bags of the supermarkets. It teaches me that things have their seasons – a very biblical idea – and helps me to appreciate the rhythm that is in life.[1] There is no doubt, too, that many vegetables grown and harvested in season taste far better than the vegetables I used to buy (they have a taste!), and so waiting brings a greater appreciation for them.

I have also grown to love the fact that my vegetables come in all different shapes and sizes with lumps and bumps. I positively dislike having to buy vegetables in the super-market: the rows of perfectly shaped and identically sized produce depresses me. How did they get like that, anyway?

One answer is that anything that does not meet the industry or supermarket standards regarding length, size, lack of blemishes and so on is thrown away. The other answer is that vegetables and fruit are produced like that through the use of chemicals: insecticides, herbicides and pesticides. Around 25,000 tonnes of pesticides were applied to UK crops in 2000 and, altogether, 430 different pesticides are permitted for use in non-organic farming.[2] The Cox's apple is a particular case in point. They can sometimes receive 36 different pesticides, through 16 sprayings. Many of these are systemic, which means they permeate into the flesh of the fruit and so cannot be removed through peeling or washing.

While these may produce big, perfect-looking vegetables,

they are damaging to the environment and to human health. There is growing concern over what has been called the 'cocktail effect': continual exposure to low levels of a variety of different chemicals, which could affect long-term health. As yet, little research has been done into this, and so possible dangers are unknown. What is known is that, because of financial gain, chemicals are often released too early into the market before proper research has been done; then, some years down the line, dangers become apparent and they have to be withdrawn. This happened, for example, with Lindane, which was made illegal in 2002, having been found to be a hormone-disrupting chemical with links to cancer.[3] The potential danger of these chemicals to babies and young children is particularly worrying, as their bodies are less able to deal with the toxic effects. It has been bringing up a child that has turned many people, including me, towards organic food.[4]

The damage being done to the environment and to bio-diversity is only too evident when you look at the difference in wildlife on organic and intensive farms. A review showed that on organic farms there were five times as many wild plants in arable fields and 57% more species. Some endangered species found on farmland were found only on organic farms. There were 44% more birds in fields outside the breeding season and, again, endangered birds such as the song thrush were significantly more numerous on organic farms. In particular, there were more than twice as many breeding skylarks.[5]

Intensive farming has been happening for only the last fifty years – the post-war period when, understandably, the rationing caused by a loss of food imports led the Government to produce a new food policy that would encourage maximum production.[6] The consumer's constant desire for cheap food has encouraged this to continue, so that since the

1950s we have seen a huge increase in production while prices have fallen. The way that our world has developed since then has allowed us to import whatever we want, whenever we want. There is no doubt that this has benefited us with cheap food all year round and an endless variety of products.

We are now beginning to realize, however, that cheap food is coming at a heavy cost. As well as the effects of intensive farming on the environment and on biodiversity, there is also the effect of the transport and the packaging involved in much of our food. It is thought that 75% of the cost of food is in its processing, packaging and distribution. We need to be aware now of 'food miles': the further a food product has travelled, the more damage it has done to the environment. With apples, for example, each kilogramme from New Zealand that is imported into the UK produces its own weight in carbon dioxide emissions.[7]

Then there are the implications for our health, and we hardly need be reminded of salmonella, BSE and the controversy over genetically modified (GM) foods.[8] Moving away from the negative, though, there are thought to be positive benefits in eating organic foods. Not enough research has been done to prove it conclusively, but tests so far suggest that organic foods tend to be higher in essential minerals and in secondary nutrients than non-organic. What is also known is that mineral levels in UK fruit and vegetables fell by up to 76% between 1940 and 1991.[9] As Michael Van Straten says, 'It seems to me a matter of common sense that food grown in rich, naturally fertilized soil will offer the optimum levels of vitamins, minerals, trace elements and ... beneficial phytonutrients'.[10]

Another important concern is that of the welfare of farmed animals. Thanks to factory farming, the meat that was most expensive when my parents were children (chicken) and the

51

meat that was most expensive when I was a child (salmon) are now among the cheapest that can be bought. When you look at the conditions in which both are produced, however, you understand why. Instead of going into the life of a battery chicken, let me quote the wonderful chef, Hugh Fearnley-Whittingstall, who says that anyone who buys such meat is 'either an idiot or a heartless bastard'.[11] The same can be said for most of the salmon that is now available, and I now try not to eat salmon unless it is from an organic farm.[12]

52   Alongside all of this is an issue of power. I do not want to create the impression that all farmers are heartless people, intent on destroying the environment. That is wrong. Many farmers care strongly for their animals and for their land, including those who are non-organic.[13] In fact, as has been well documented, farming is in a crisis. While 2002/3 showed patchy improvement, in 2001/2 the average farmer earned just under £10,000, and there were nearly 60,000 job losses from 1998 to 2001.[14] No, the problem lies with those who control what happens in farming: the biotechnology companies who produce the pesticides; the big food manufacturers, who can influence what kind of food is grown; and the supermarkets that control distribution and dictate prices and uniformity of produce (Tesco, Sainsbury's, Asda and Safeway account for 75% of all UK grocery sales). Pivotal to these is the Government, which should be better involved in issues of food labelling, safety standards and supporting good farming practices.[15]

As Wendell Berry says, how and what we eat is a political issue – an issue of freedom.

There is a politics of food that, like any politics, involves our freedom. We still (sometimes) remember that we cannot be free if our minds and voices are controlled by someone else. But we have neglected to understand that we cannot be free if our food and our sources are controlled by someone else. The condition of the passive consumer of food is not a democratic condition. One reason to eat responsibly is to eat free.[16]

Our attitude to food is determined by other aspects of our lives. When we look at 'S is for Simplicity' we shall see the importance of time and how our use of time reflects our values and affects many areas of our lives. This is no less true with regards to food, and there is a clear relationship between food and time. Biblically, food is a part of the gift relationship that God established with humanity in the Garden of Eden. We see there the goodness of food as a gift from God to sustain us, and this is reflected in the way we use food as a central part of our relationship-building. Our demand for convenience, as seen already in 'D is for Driving', threatens to erode the relational aspect of food.[17]

There is thus a spiritual side to food. See how often the Bible links food and eating with central biblical concepts (communion, the water of life, fasting, 'taste and see that the LORD is good', the eschatological banquet and so on). Michael Schut views food as a sacrament and talks of 'the spirituality embodied in our personal and cultural relationship to food'.[18] I see the food I eat as one of the ways in which I worship God, eating in a manner that respects what he has created, both human and non-human.

Action points

- Buy local, organic food and try to buy as little as possible from the supermarket. At present, 70% of organic food is imported, with all the consequent issues of transportation and packaging. Farm shops, delivery boxes and Farmers' Markets are great ways to do this. (The Soil Association provides information on these.) If you have to choose, go local rather than organic, but try to do both!

- Grow your own food. Whether you have an allotment or just a windowsill, you can grow some of your own things, helping to make the connection between your food and the land. You will know exactly what has gone into it and the food miles are zero.

- Find out your supermarket's policies on becoming GM-free, being more open about levels of pesticides, stocking local, organic food, reducing food waste and unnecessary packaging, stocking fairly traded products and buying meat and dairy products from farms that do not regularly use antibiotics. (Contact Friends of the Earth's 'Real Food Campaign' for more details and see 'B is for Bananas' for more on fair trade.) Let them know what you would like their policies to be ('L is for Letters' looks more at how you can do this).

Good contacts
Compassion in World Farming: Charles House, 5a Charles St, Petersfield, Hampshire GU32 3EH; 01730 264208; <www.ciwf.co.uk>
Friends of the Earth (see 'C is for Creation').
National Farmers Union: Agriculture House, 164 Shaftesbury Avenue, London WC2H 8HL; 020 7331 7200; <www.nfu.org.uk>
The Soil Association: Bristol House, 40–56 Victoria St, Bristol BS1 6BY; 0117 929 0661; <www.soilassociation.org>

Good books
J. Blythe, *The Food Our Children Eat*
H. Fearnley-Whittingstall, *The River Cottage Cookbook*
J. Humphrys, *The Great Food Gamble*

G is for Globalization [1]

'Let's see how many countries we represent today,' I asked the people in my seminar. 'Have a look at the clothes you're wearing, the bag you're carrying, the palmtop you're using, the pen you're writing with, and see where they all come from.' As people called out, it soon became clear that we were wearing and using things from all around the world: jeans from Morocco, a pen from Malaysia, a palmtop assembled in the Philippines, an apple from New Zealand, a bag from Bali, a diary from China.

In 'A is for Activists' we looked at what it means to be people who want to spend themselves on behalf of the hungry and satisfy the needs of the oppressed (Is. 58:10). If we are to work effectively in our world, we need to understand the context in which our world is set.

This is where the word 'globalization' comes in. There are certain words that sum up the story that people find themselves in and that give people meaning and a way to understand the world. As Ian Linden puts it, 'today the word "globalization" encapsulates our latest contemporary story'.[2] The Department for International Development (DFID) provides a good definition of globalization as being simply 'the process by which the world is becoming more and more connected and interdependent'.[3] People's answers in the seminar I was leading on globalization proved the point. In particular, since the events of 11 September 2001, we are realizing how interlinked we are with the rest of our world.

The word 'globalization' generates huge debate between those who are for it and those who are against it. Globalization is bound up with the theory of free-trade market capitalism (that is, trade liberalization, privatization and financial market deregulation). The 'pro-globalizers' believe free trade between nations, with no protective barriers, to be the most effective way of increasing global wealth and of lifting poorer countries out of poverty. It is incontestable that market capitalism has led to increasing global wealth, as the proportion of GDP traded internationally has risen from 5% in 1946 to 25% now.[4] The Sachs/Warner study from Harvard University found that developing countries with open economies grew by 4.5% a year in the 1970s and 1980s, while those with closed economies grew by 0.7% a year.[5]

Pro-globalizers regard those who argue against globalization as idealistic and naïve, and as failing to understand the complexities and ultimate benefits of the financial system. They believe that those who would stop markets acting efficiently (by making a special case for poor countries) will in the end destroy the wealth of those nations. Take, for example, flower-growers in Uganda, who produce flowers for export to Europe. It is hard work, but it pays better than subsistence farming. Not only do Europeans get flowers in winter but the Ugandans eat better and are able to school their children.[6] In other words, it may be a tough option but in the long run joining world markets is the only way to create wealth.[7] Such people also argue that many countries are held back, not by unfair terms of trade, but by internal corruption or by the lack of an economic infrastructure that would allow them to deliver the goods in world markets.[8]

'Anti-globalizers' see the gap between rich and poor widening and blame the growth of global capitalism for that gap. Thus we have the situation today whereby more than 800 million people do not have enough to eat and where the income gap between the top and bottom fifths of the world's people jumped from 30:1 in 1960 to 74:1 in 1997.

Our Ugandan flower-growers would question whether, overall, they are better off. Yes, they might have more money, but they now have to buy the basic goods they would have grown, which are now sold more expensively because demand is high. They are now at the mercy of market prices, and the chemicals they use to grow the flowers are threatening both their lands and their health. They might also ask why there was subsistence farming in the first place.

People on this side of the debate point out that the collapse of communism has led to a much more ruthless kind of capitalism. They see that the way to change the operation of multinationals is by exposing their practices in the press and by protesting publicly about their power. This side of the debate wants massive intervention to stop poverty caused by capitalism, and wants partnerships between nation states, charities (non-governmental organizations; NGOs), multinationals and global agencies to bring about reform.[9]

Pro-globalizers point to the massive benefits that globalization has brought us: freedom of movement, freedom of communication, freedom of consumer choice. Anti-globalizers talk about the 'McDonaldization' of the world; the rearing of the 'MTV generation' and the recognition of Nike and Disney as global symbols. Naomi Klein calls this the 'branding of culture':[10] there is no space left any more that does not have a brand name attached to it. Every thing and every event comes at a price and with a logo (usually American). Pro-globalizers say this is rubbish; America does not hold the corporate power that is claimed. Furthermore, branding is not the manipulating evil that it is made out to be. Human beings have minds of their own and can choose what they do and do not buy.

The debate remains polarized and the arguments are often

highly complex and technical. The reality, though, is that there is a middle ground that is trodden more often than is sometimes thought. Many anti-globalizers are not actually anti-globalization as such, but are against the current effects of economic globalization as presently managed by the International Monetary Fund, the World Bank and the WTO.[11] Similarly, a commentator such as Philippe Legrain, coming from a staunchly free-trade position, would still advocate the need for debt cancellation, reform of the WTO, increased aid, capital controls, and for governments to do more to protect the vulnerable when people lose out from globalization.[12]

58

One thing is clear: in our increasingly globalized world, the different issues involved in the problem must be seen as part of the wider whole, rather than as separate. As Peter Heslam says, 'The interests of the environment, economic growth, security and democracy are diverse but also interconnected and therefore need to be treated together, rather than in isolation.'[13]

Technology has ensured that globalization is here to stay.[14] Capitalism seems to be the best way forward for generating wealth, and no viable alternatives are being proposed. The key is to channel globalization rather than to demand its demise: to channel it so that the rights of local people and their environment come before the rights of shareholders to increase their profits. As we have seen in 'B is for Bananas', two things are paramount here: one is the reform of the WTO so that this becomes its overriding principle,[15] and the second, related to it, is the establishment of a system of accountability for corporations whereby they would adopt best practice in their work and be accountable for any environmental and social damage.[16]

As we saw at the beginning of this chapter, globalization defines our world today. In many ways, this whole book could be seen as looking at how to respond to globalization.

(Almost all the issues we are discussing, and many of the action points, relate directly to it.) But does the Bible have any relevance here?

Most positively, it needs to be stated again that there is nothing wrong, *per se*, with globalization. In fact, the Bible, too, has a global vision. Whether it is the foundational call of Abram (Gen. 12:3), the words of the prophets (e.g. Is. 49:6), the universality of Jesus' message (e.g. Matt. 8:11) or the inclusivity of Paul (Rom. 14:11), we see a vision of the peoples of the world united in worshipping the God who made them.

It is in the book of Revelation that we see the vision in all its glory with its picture of the throne of God, before which is 'a great multitude that no-one could count, from every nation, tribe, people and language' (7:9).[17] At the heart of this scene is Jesus, the Lamb; the biblical vision finds its centre and fulfilment in him.

One of the implications of this universality of the Bible is that it goes right against globalization's treatment of culture. Globalization is often seen as a promotion of American culture and as playing a part in destroying local cultures. As the Bible unfolds, however, it is clear that there is no sacred culture or language. Every culture is acceptable and valid as a vehicle for God's revelation.[18] This both relativizes and gives value to individual cultures in a way that globalization does not.

While globalization itself might be neutral, the biblical vision demonstrates that Christians have a global dream that is far more fulfilling than that offered by globalization. As Alex Araujo says, 'globalization is the current strategy that a secular and lost humanity has developed to cope with an existence devoid of faith and hope in God'.[19]

Tom Sine is particularly clear on the need to show people the Christian hope that can be brought to a world caught in the clutches of globalization and claims that 'the only way we can begin to contend with the seductions of McWorld is to offer a more compelling dream than the Western Dream'. This dream is of a new heaven and a new earth 'in which justice comes for the poor, the instruments of warfare are transformed into the instruments of peace and festive banqueting and celebration will welcome us home'.

Action point

- Look at the food you buy, the clothes you wear, the equipment you use. Where is it from? Develop an awareness of the interconnectedness of your life with other people and environments all over the world.

Good books

P. Legrain, *Open World: The Truth about Globalization*
A. Roddick (ed.), *Take It Personally: How Globalization Affects You and Powerful Ways to Challenge It*
J. Stiglitz, *Globalization and Its Discontents*

H is for HIV

What was the single biggest killer among women aged 25–39 years in New York in the 1980s?[1] Amazingly, it wasn't cancer or homicide, but Aids, which has become the most destructive disease humanity has ever seen, infecting over 60 million people. In Sub-Saharan Africa, it is the leading cause of death and, worldwide, is the fourth-biggest killer. It is thought that Aids will eventually kill half of all 15-year-old Ethiopian, South African and Zimbabwean boys. At the end of 2001, 40 million people were estimated to be HIV+ (HIV positive).[2]

Transmission of the virus occurs in three ways: through intimate sexual contact; by infected blood entering the bloodstream and from the HIV+ mother to her baby. While Aids was initially labelled a 'gay disease', this was in fact a serious distortion of the truth. Today, the majority of new infections are among heterosexual women aged between 15 and 24. In Africa, for every 10 men infected there are 12 or 13 women. Incredibly, in one area in South Africa, 58% of women aged between 20 and 24 are HIV+.[3] In Botswana and some other parts of southern Africa, more than 30% of pregnant women are infected.

The numbers are immense, but in each of those numbers is the individual suffering that must be borne by every person who contracts HIV and by every person who sees a loved one die from it. The psychological effects of the trauma cannot begin to be envisaged.

One of the key problems is the huge numbers of orphans that this disease is causing. Since the beginning, 13.2 million children have been orphaned. Of these 13.2 million, 10% have the Aids virus themselves. This places enormous strain on the wider family, particularly on the grandparents, who, in their old age, might find themselves having to support as many as thirty grandchildren. In Botswana, every income earner in the poorest quarter of households can expect to take on four more dependants.

Not surprisingly, therefore, HIV/Aids has huge economic implications. The workforce of some African nations is being devastated as people cannot work, either through having the virus or through having to care for those who do. This is deeply affecting the annual per capita growth of Sub-Saharan Africa in particular. It is thought that 20% of GDP could be lost by 2020 in those countries most heavily affected.

In recognition of this, businesses have to factor in the financial implications of a high turnover of staff and the increasing costs of training, insurance and benefits. The International Labour Organization predicts that by 2020 the workforce of Namibia will have fallen by 22%. The falling workforce will have dire results on the production of staple foods: the Zimbabwe Farmers Union predicts that Aids will reduce national maize production by 61% and vegetables by 49%.[4]

What is clear in all of this is that Aids is directly linked with poverty. Everything that has been said so far shows how it leads *to* poverty, but it is becoming increasingly recognized that poverty is also one of its main causes.

Medicine is expensive, controlled by pharmaceutical firms from the wealthier countries. The struggle to pay for it is either impossible or strips families of money that should go on food and education. As one Zimbabwean doctor put it, 'Drug companies are only really interested in us as a potential market and though our need is great we don't count as consumers because we can't afford to pay their prices.' She went on to say, 'As a doctor it is hard for me to know that my patients may die of treatable diseases because our community cannot afford the medication. Imagine the pain a mother feels watching her child die of pneumonia, knowing that if she lived another life, if she had transport to the nearest clinic, if she could buy the drugs herself, the child might survive.'[5]

Many healthcare systems in general are struggling, and this leads to a greater risk of infection as other sexually transmitted diseases (STDs) are ignored. Once someone is infected with HIV, a lack of medicine increases the likelihood of other infections. When the future looks hopeless, there seems little point in taking care with life; and young people do not take, and are unable to take, the necessary precautions.[6]

UNAIDS (the Joint United Nations Programme on HIV/ AIDS) describes Aids as 'an index of existing social and economic injustices', and it is interesting, bearing in mind our previous chapter on globalization, how many of the factors involved in the globalizing of our world find expression in the Aids crisis. Gary Paterson expresses it well: 'A society's vulnerability to HIV/Aids is closely bound up with its lack of ability to resist global economic forces, including the results of structural adjustment, the debt burden, privatization of services, and WTO policies on intellectual property rights, trade and services.'[7]

63

Because of this, UNAIDS' writings on what would be an effective response to help a nation reverse infection trends identify debt relief as being a key. Alongside debt relief there needs to be a recognition of how the policies of the WTO, the IMF and the World Bank have an impact on the poorest people and on HIV transmission rates. In order for this to happen there must be strong political support and leadership on these issues.

It is well recognized, but not always applied, that one of the main ways to tackle the situation is prevention through education because, alongside poverty, promiscuity is a key factor in the spread of the virus. In particular, education should be targeted at young people, many of whom know precious little about Aids. In some countries, UNICEF estimates that over 50% of young people aged 15 to 24 have never heard of Aids or do not know enough to prevent infection.

Alongside young people, the education of women is also vital in controlling infection rates, and this is another example of how women's rights play a central role in development. Adrienne Germain, president of the International Women's Health Coalition for the UN, says that 'men's demands for sex' are to blame, not any ignorance or promiscuity on the part of women: 'it is because men have sex with any number of women – and they bring it back to their wives'.[8] Empowering women to be able to say no to sex, or at least to insist on the use of a condom, is essential.

It is interesting to note Catherine von Ruhland's comment that 'the transmission of Aids is wholly preventable and so a change in behaviour could wipe out the virus in a generation'.[9] Education needs to take place on a number of issues, including looking at safer drug-injecting behaviour. Most important, however, is the need to educate on safer sexual behaviour. The World Health Organization has stated that

> ... the most effective way to prevent the sexual transmission of HIV is to abstain from sexual intercourse or for two uninfected partners to remain mutually faithful. Sexual relationships that do not include sexual intercourse can lessen the risk of HIV transmission. The risk of spreading HIV through sexual intercourse can be significantly reduced by the proper and consistent use of condoms.[10]

Finally, responses to the crisis (whether prevention or care) are always most effective where they are local and community-based. In particular, these should involve those who are actually HIV+ themselves. In order for this and for any of the above to happen, we need to foster social openness and be fighting against the stigmatism and prejudice that surround HIV/Aids.

This brings us right back home, because we cannot see Aids as something that is affecting only poorer countries. While the majority of cases are elsewhere (the UK infection figure is 0.11%), we cannot get complacent. One of the reasons the UK is low down on the scale is because of the massive education programmes that happened in the late 1980s and the initiatives since then that have worked so hard at breaking the stigmatism attached to the virus. But education needs to happen in each generation if it is to maintain its effectiveness.

The HIV issue touches on many biblical principles. We see it reflected in Jesus' refusal to bow down to the social conventions of his day, and in his compassion for those who were stigmatized and outcast (e.g. the man with leprosy, Mark 1:40–42). We see it reflected in the Old Testament's belief that the right of all to use the Earth's resources comes before anyone's right to ownership (see 'C is for Creation'), and medicine must surely be a modern-day application of that. We see it reflected in the value that the Bible gives to women (particularly within marriage: 1 Cor. 7:3–5) and to fidelity within marriage (Matt. 5:27–32). Perhaps most especially, we see the HIV crisis reflected in the biblical injunction to have a particular concern for the widow and the orphan (e.g. Deut. 24:17–21; Jas. 1:27). Whether through education, care or campaigning, there is much that we can do, nationally and internationally, to be responding to that call.

65

Action points [11]

- Protest about WTO, IMF and World Bank policies that keep poverty as the driving force behind the spread of HIV. The organizations given in 'A is for Activists' will be helpful here.

- Pray for the advancement of research and for those people infected and affected.

- Promote and support the work of charities that work in this area (see below).

Good contacts

ACET UK: PO Box 3693, London SW15 2BQ; 020 8780 0400; <www.acetuk.org>; <acet@acetuk.org>

HopeHIV: PO Box 1190, Kingston and Surbiton KT2 6LB; 020 8288 1196; <www.hopehiv.org>

I is for Investments

In the Cleethorpes and Grimsby area, CARE (Christian Action and Resource Enterprise) works to offer practical help and advice to those who are in need. They have a charity shop that provides jobs and training for those hoping to re-enter employment and receives donated household goods that can be sold or given to needy families. They also help in the areas of debt and welfare rights and provide a rent scheme that helps to house families.

Far away, in Chile, the cooperative Liberación is a savings and loan bank that promotes and strengthens small businesses and helps to create jobs; while, in Kenya, the Family Finance Building Society works with women and children in rural and slum areas, setting up micro-credit programmes to stimulate employment. Back in the UK, again, Organic South West is a regional advisory centre for farmers, growers and businesses, helping them with all aspects of the organic market.[1]

All of these businesses have recently received loans, to help them improve their work, from a bank attempting to operate on an ethical basis. Perhaps my money has played a part in the work they do?

In contrast, in one part of the world a corporation's

activities is destroying the livelihoods of the indigenous people in order to increase shareholder profits, while in a nearby village in the UK another local bank branch closes down. Perhaps my money has allowed this to happen?

Through this book we are looking at how we can use our lives to help the world. The good news is that what we do with our money can play a significant part in that. For those of us who are rich (compared to most of the world's population), actively seeking to do good with our money isn't just a responsibility: it's a definite blessing!

In a later chapter we shall look more fully at the wider subject of money. The principle guiding this chapter, though, is that the question of money is not just about how much we give, but also about what we do with what we keep. From this perspective, the topic of investments, for those of us who are in a position to have surplus money to invest, is a very important one that cannot be ignored.

Most of us reading this book will have savings and investments in one form or another. That might mean just a current account, or we may have invested in the stock market. We may have TESSAs or ISAs, National Savings or bonds. The majority of us will, at some point in our lives, have a mortgage and a pension.

The first questions to ask are: Should a Christian have investments in the first place and, if so, what is an appropriate level?[2] Does saving anything demonstrate a lack of faith in God's provision, or does *not* saving demonstrate a lack of prudence and good stewardship? The Bible seems to teach both (compare Prov. 6:8; 21:20 with Matt. 6:19). Lest we answer too quickly that Jesus' teaching should always come before that of the Old Testament, we should not forget that he himself depended on the support of wealthy women and did not demand that Nicodemus or Joseph of Arimathea give all their money away in order to be his disciples.

There would seem to be two positive grounds given in the Bible for savings: first, we save in order to fulfil our family obligations (Mark. 7:9–13; 1 Tim. 5:8) and, secondly, we save in order not to be dependent on anyone (2 Thess. 3:6–12), and in our society that would include the State. Alongside this is the continual and overarching reminder that we must use any money or possessions we have to help the poor (e.g. Eph. 4:28). Nowhere does the Bible say we should invest simply to gain more money in order to become more financially secure!

This does, of course, still leave room for interpretation as to what that means. How far does our family extend? How much should we leave our children? How much do we need to live on in order to avoid dependence? In this, as with so much, the Bible's teaching gives us parameters but not a single, universally applicable norm. The appropriate attitude to wealth would seem to depend to some extent on the Christian's situation and calling (for instance, to the mission field, to a dependent family, to singleness, and so on).

What we need to remember at all times is our natural inclination to justify saving the most we can. We must always guard ourselves against the desire to accumulate as much as possible in order to make ourselves as secure as possible.

Beyond this, though, a further question to ask is *how* should we save: what forms should our investments take?[3] Surprisingly, the Bible provides a fair amount of guidance on this matter. Stewardship of our money, as well as of the rest of creation, is a key principle: taking personal responsibility ourselves, not just letting others have control of our finances for us, and also ensuring that any business activity we are involved with promotes the welfare of creation. Relationships are always central and placed above the accumulation of wealth. Accountability and openness are important, therefore, so that we know to what purposes our savings are being put. By contrast with our interest-based society, the Bible does place an absolute ban on all interest.[4] Finally, as we shall see more fully in 'M is for Money', the Bible is clear that no money should be acquired at the expense of someone else or through dishonesty.

If these principles are followed, it will be apparent how starkly they stand in opposition to the accepted forms of investment that the majority of us as Christians follow today. For example, we too often hold shares in large companies where there is no local accountability or relational basis and where interest is used as the means of making profit. Banks, likewise, give depositors no control over the use of their finances or over the way the bank conducts its relationships with its borrowers.[5]

Perhaps most important for the purposes of this book is the fact that so much of conventional saving today is in companies that exploit their customers, their workers and the created world. As Christians we have a responsibility to see where our money is going and to ensure that it is not being used to the detriment of other people or of the environment.

The reality is that there are all sorts of things that our money might be being used for if it is invested in the conventional ways (some of which might not cause you personally a problem). It might be being used for the production and sale of military hardware or nuclear power. It might be being donated to a political party or involved in pornography, the fur trade or tobacco production. It could be being used by an oppressive regime that tramples on human rights. It could be involved in intensive farming, environmentally destructive mining, illegal felling of tropical hardwoods, or water pollution. Our money could be used for currency speculation, which can damage a nation's economy, or it might still be used to service a southern country's debt. Our money has a lot of power, and there are so many things we can do with it. In the light of this we must be aware of where our money might be going.

Thankfully, we *can* do something about this and we *can* control what happens with our money, if we are prepared to put in a little bit of time and not automatically accept what we are told. 'Ethical' or 'socially responsible' investments are on the rise and are increasingly easy to come by for all investment purposes, including mortgages and pensions.[6]

The term 'ethical investments' covers a fairly broad spectrum, and we need always to do our own work to see if a particular investment option meets our specific ethical criteria. Some options work 'negatively' (by not investing in particular concerns such as the arms trade or tobacco) whereas other options work 'positively' (investing only in companies that are specifically working for social or environmental enhancement). One good point to look for is openness and transparency in how an investment option works. For example, Triodos Bank produces a regular newsletter for its investors that gives details of some of the different businesses and projects to which it is lending.

Some of us may be in a position to go further than using only these 'ethical middlemen'. 'Business angels' are people who invest money and become shareholders in small businesses, and often are able to give advice and expertise too. This must be one of the best ways to invest any extra money we might have: there is a good balance of risk and return; close relationships are often fostered and this helps us to know exactly where our money is going, thus enhancing our role as stewards.

However we choose to play it, the key is that, whenever we put some money into an account, invest in an ISA, apply for a mortgage and so on, we have a direct opportunity to use our money to do some good in our world: and that can only be an exciting thing.

Action points

- Look at where your money is invested. Is it being used for good or to harm?

- Take time to look into the different ethical options that are on offer (see below).

- Choose one area in which you can change where your money is being invested and make that change. Remember when you do so to inform your bank, mortgage lender or pension scheme manager (etc.) why you are changing. When you have done that, choose another area to change, and so on. Don't try to rush this process: give yourself time to make the changes slowly if that is what you need.

Good contacts[7]

The Co-operative Bank plc: 0800 905090;
<www.co-operativebank.co.uk>
EIRIS (Ethical Investment Research Service): 504 Bondway Business Centre, 71 Bondway, London SW8 1SQ; 0171 735 1351; <www.eiris.org>
Ethical Consumer magazine (see 'B is for Bananas')
Shared Interest: 25 Collingwood Street, Newcastle NE1 1JE; 0191 233 9100; <www.shared-interest.com>
Triodos Bank: Brunel House, 11 The Promenade, Bristol BS8 3NN; 0800 328 2181; <www.tridos.co.uk>

J is for Jobs

Do you leap out of bed on a Monday morning, thrilled to be able to start another week's paid work, and do you come home on a Friday evening, despondent because the week is over? Perhaps not!

Maybe, though, you are wondering what the subject of jobs has to do with this book. Well, this is where we begin to move into the area of simplicity, something that we shall look at further in 'S is for Simplicity'. At its most basic, the idea of simplicity speaks for itself. It is about simplifying our lives in the face of our society's constant demands. It is about developing a life of awareness and rhythm that enables us to focus on our relationships with God, with one another and with the created world.

What simplicity teaches us is that being involved in God's heart for justice is not only about the specific things we do in that area, such as ethical investments and campaigning. Rather, it is a holistic thing that encompasses every area of our lives. For many of us, work (including travel) can take up 60% or 70% of our waking hours. It is what the biggest portion of our lives is given over to, and the thing that more than anything else can inform who we are.

The first thing that we need to recognize is the difference between employment (including self-employment) and work (which can include voluntary work, that done by carers, and so on). Both contribute to the wider community; one is paid while the other is not. There are a number of different reasons for paid employment: earning money; gaining a sense of security; tradition; enjoyment; duty; to serve others; learning; prestige and status; socializing; personal growth; success; creativity; fulfilment ... Which of these apply to you? More broadly, work has two functions: the financial and the personal. For some of us, both of these functions may be met in our jobs. For others, our job may meet the financial need primarily, and the other types of reward are found in unpaid activities.[1]

Considering our jobs in this way helps to free us from the fatalistic sense that we *have* to do whatever job we are currently doing, and opens our eyes to other possibilities. Why are we doing what we are doing? Is it what we want to do? Is it what we believe God is calling us to do? Did we decide to take this career path because of the cultural expectations around us? Is our job a result of decisions made, years ago, that we didn't even realize we were making?

Some of us have got ourselves caught up in the materialistic rat race that so many are running. Ellen Goodman sums this up well: 'Normal is getting dressed in clothes that you buy for work, driving through traffic in a car that you are still paying for, in order to get to the job you need so you can pay for the clothes, car and the house that you leave empty all day in order to afford to live in it.'[2]

Looking at our work in this way gives us the opportunity to reappraise the jobs we are in and ask ourselves if there are any changes that we want to begin to make.

John's story is a good example. He was a City lawyer, specializing in the investigation of international bank fraud, when he was first challenged about the claims of the Christian faith by a barrister. Three years of forensic investigation later, he accepted that what was written in the Gospels was true. But it made no difference, of course, because an intellectual faith is in reality no faith. He was in Hong Kong on a fraud

73

investigation and heard the testimonies of some of the ex-heroin-addict former Triad gangsters who worked with Jackie Pullinger. It was their tales that brought it home to him that if Christ had risen, he was alive and at work today. Then everything changed, and John left law to go and work with Jackie Pullinger. While working there, he felt God calling him back to the UK; and in time he set up a bank, working with people who are keen to come off benefits and to stand on their own feet. From a large house in an upmarket part of London, he and his family moved to a bungalow in a run-down area and their time was given to home-schooling their children and working with people in need. John's story is not about moving from a non-Christian to a Christian option: investigating international bank fraud could be a high Christian calling. Rather, what John's story illustrates is his willingness to change in the light of what he felt God was asking of him.

While this kind of lifestyle change may be an option for some, for the majority of us our jobs simply help us to keep our heads above water. Work in the UK is currently in crisis as people find themselves working longer and longer hours. In fact, Britons work the longest hours of any country in the EU. Research shows that many managers have no time for other interests and believe that their work damages their health, as well as affecting their relationships with their children and partner.[3]

Our society is characterized by an unprecedented stress on work. This links back with what we have seen about globalization and looks forward to 'M is for Money' and 'N is for Needs', in which we shall see the central place that growth and money have in our culture. We live in a world of skewed values in which human fulfilment is seen as being an escape from work and a necessity, but in which the means to do this is still human work and achievement. We work in order to increase our wealth, in order to achieve leisure.[4] Work is thus rarely seen as an end in itself.

This is in direct contrast with the biblical testimony. Here, work (whether paid or unpaid) is good in and of itself: something that God ordained for people to do. In Genesis 1:26–28 and 9:7 we see that God made us to work. Work is an indispensable part of what it means to be human, and even God himself is described as doing work (Gen. 2:2 and elsewhere). Work is thus an important aspect of our self-fulfilment as people, rather than something to be avoided at all costs.[5] The search for excellence and achievement is not disparaged, but positively encouraged (as seen, for example, in the building of the tabernacle in Exod. 35).

At the same time, however, work is not the means to salvation; and there is a negative side to it, as seen in the curse of the fall. Work can be hard and painful and, certainly, it can be used for wrong ends rather than positive creativity.

We need also to remember that work is not the be-all and end-all: God's week of creation finished with a day to rest. Our lives should have a rhythm to them that includes time set aside to rest and time that is specifically dedicated to worshipping God. Our calling (our 'vocation', if you like) is not limited to work; it also includes friendship, play, love, worship and rest.[6]

Because of faulty theologies that have permeated the church (particularly those that created a sacred–secular divide) we have seen our workplaces as places where we have to go in order to survive, as opposed to our churches, which is where the *real* work of being a Christian takes place. Thus we may spend many hours of our day working in the supermarket, but it's the two hours that we spend running the youth work that get the attention. Instead of this, we need to develop what Mark Greene describes as 'faith consciousness':

a deliberate awareness of God's presence in our workplaces and an integration of our faith, our work and the rest of our lives.[7]

The challenges that our workplaces give us are many. We might find ourselves working in areas that perpetuate the problems that we are looking at in this book, and the rightness, or otherwise, of our staying there is hard to consider. One of the most satisfying and frustrating aspects of Christianity is that in so many areas of life there are no hard-and-fast rules, but guidelines to follow and the Holy Spirit to prompt. This applies here too. God will call some of us to work within the structures that perpetuate the injustices we have looked at so far in this book. Look at Daniel. Look at Joseph. This is no easy calling: it comes accompanied by its own pressures and frustrations, working out where compromise is the right route and where it is not. Others of us God will call to find work that brings us outside the structures. Look at Amos. Both positions will give us opportunities to critique and to live and speak prophetically; but, wherever we stand, we must do so knowing that this is where God has placed us.

Action points

- Is there is an attitude about your work that you need to change? Do you know that you are where God has placed you?

- Is there some way in which you might be able to help your place of work become more socially and environmentally friendly?

Good contacts

Administry: The Mega Centre, Bernard Road, Sheffield S2 5BQ; 0114 278 0090; <www.administry.co.uk>

London Institute for Contemporary Christianity: St Peter's,
Vere Street, London W1G 0DQ; 020 7399 9555;
<www.licc.org.uk>

A good book
M. Greene, *Thank God it's Monday: Ministry in the
     Workplace*

K is for Kippers

Our local fish-'n'-chip shop informs its customers that all its
cod comes from Icelandic waters and not from the North Sea.
When I talked with the owner he told me that he had made a
point of insisting that this was where his supplies came from.
So many people had asked him about it, and he had seen his
sales starting to fall; so he realized that he had better do
something about it.

The saga of the humble cod has become a symbol for what is
happening in our seas. At the beginning of 2003 it hit the news
again with the release of the 'State of the World's Fisheries and
Aquaculture 2002' report (SOFIA). The report states that nearly
half of the world's marine stocks have been fully exploited and
there is no expectation that they will expand again. In
particular, cod levels in the North Sea (from where our fish-
'n'-chip-loving nation has traditionally got its cod) are at their
lowest ever and seem in danger of complete collapse.

The modern practice of trawling (whereby weighted nets are dragged across the sea floor to catch prawns and bottom-dwelling fish) is one of the main reasons for the decline of fish stocks. Trawling destroys the thick natural carpet of plants and animals that live on the floor and that is necessary for the survival of the fry of fish such as cod. Not only this, but trawling is indiscriminate in what it catches; it can damage or destroy species such as corals and sponges that take years to recolonize.[1] Prawn trawling is of particular concern, since it is responsible for one-third of the world's discarded catch, and up to 25% of seabed life can be removed by the pass of just one prawn trawl.[2]

In fact, our seas and oceans are facing many serious threats, all of which come from land-based activities that we are often directly involved with.[3] Some of these problems we have seen already in previous chapters, such as climate change (among other things, the melting of ice-caps could change whole ecosystems and cause low-lying land to be lost), pollution from intensive agriculture (and also from chemical and pharmaceutical manufacturing) and oil pollution.[4]

In 'W is for Water' we shall look further at the problem of sewage, but here it is worth noting that 912 million litres of industrial and domestic sewage (24%) is discharged untreated into natural waters in the UK. Such high levels of untreated sewage are toxic to fish and can cause eutrophication, a process of nutrient-enrichment that deoxygenates the water, literally suffocating the species in it. A further threat comes from the huge amount of litter that we generate and that finds its way into the sea. Plastic, in particular, is a problem; an estimated million seabirds and 100,000 sea mammals and turtles die every year from entanglement in, or ingestion of, plastics.

Returning to our kippers, the global fishing industry is huge; it was worth $55.2 billion in 2000.[5] The most significant feature of the modern fishing industry is the rise in aquaculture, where fish and seafood are farmed rather than being caught wild. Aquaculture is the fastest-growing sector of all animal food production, growing from 3.9% of fish supplies in 1970 to 29% (48.2 million tonnes) in 2001. On average, it has grown by 9.2% a year since 1970, compared with meat production, which has grown by only 2.8%.[6]

Around a third of the fish and seafood we buy will have been raised in fish farms, and this proportion is growing as we demand increasing amounts of fish and seafood in the face of declining wild stocks. Since salmon and prawns are two farmed species that are particularly popular in the UK, it is helpful to look more closely at what is involved in their production.

As was pointed out in 'F is for Food', salmon has moved from being a luxury that few could afford to being one of the cheapest of meats, filling the supermarket shelves and available at any restaurant. In Scotland, the fish-farm industry is now worth £260 million. But this is coming at a price.[7] One key concern is the amount of chemicals that are used in salmon-rearing. Around thirty different chemicals are licensed for use on fish farms, including an artificial pigment that is given in order to make the naturally grey flesh pink. Since 1997, Government scientists have detected chemicals including DDT, as well as the listeria bacterium and a mould, aflatoxin, in farmed salmon. Salmon-farming is very polluting because old water containing high concentrations of chemicals and fish faeces is flushed out in exchange for new. Since 1996 there have been 35 pollution incidents involving fish-farm effluent in the UK. In 2000/2001, 10,000 km^3 of Scotland's west coast were closed to scallop-fishing due to high levels of Amnesic Shellfish Poisoning. During the summer of 2000, 57 of the 60 areas closed were in salmon-farming areas.[8]

Above, we saw the damaging effects of prawn-trawling; and unfortunately current farming practices are not much better.[9] Some of the issues are similar to those regarding salmon; prawns are farmed intensively, using high levels of feed, pesticides, antibiotics and other chemicals in order to maximize profits and combat disease. The resultant pollution is horrendous. In Thailand, prawn ponds discharge around 1.3 billion m^3 of effluent into coastal waters each year. Of particular concern is the loss of coastal habitats and the damage done to nearby marine ecosystems such as coral reefs. Mangrove swamps in Africa and South-east Asia have been cleared in a manner similar to the clear-cutting of the rainforests (see 'P is for Paper') in order to make room for prawn ponds. From 1987 to 1993 Thailand lost more than 17% of its mangrove forests to ponds. This degradation has left coastal areas exposed to erosion, flooding and storm damage, altered natural drainage patterns, increased salt intrusion and removed critical habitats for many aquatic and terrestrial species. Ironically, 2 kg of fishmeal (often sourced from low-value fish caught wild) is needed to produce 1 kg of farmed prawns.

The good news is that our supermarkets are taking notice of some of these issues and the majority of them now source their cod and haddock from sustainable fisheries (i.e. line-caught from Icelandic waters). They still have a long way to go, however – particularly regarding salmon and prawns – and it is up to us as their customers to help them along the way. The health benefits of eating fish are well known and hence demand is growing. In the creation story we are told that God caused the water to 'teem with living creatures' and blessed those creatures and commanded them to be 'fruitful and increase in number and fill the water in the seas' (Gen. 1:20–22). We can be extremely thankful that he did so, as there is no doubting the delight of eating those fruits of the sea. Whether we enjoy them from the supermarket or at the restaurant, we must take responsibility to ensure that our pleasure is not working against that blessing and coming at the expense of God's world.

Action points
- Ask your supermarket where the fish and seafood you buy comes from. Congratulate them where they are getting it right and ask them to change where they are getting it wrong.

- Develop an awareness of how your activities might impact the seas, however far away they seem. See 'F is for Food' and 'R is for Recycling' for more information on intensive farming, plastics and sanitary products.

Good contacts
Environmental Justice Foundation: 5 St Peter's Street, London N1 8JD; 020 7359 0440; <www.ejfoundation.org>
Food and Agriculture Organization of the United Nations (FAO): Viale delle Terme di Caracalla, 00100, Rome, Italy; <www.fao.org>
Marine Conservation Society: 9 Gloucester Road, Ross-on-Wye, Herefordshire HR9 5BY; 01989 566017; <www.mcsuk.org>

A good book
Marine Conservation Society, *Good Fish Guide*

L is for Letters

'Oh, no! Here's another one from that Mrs Valerio again ... !'

I sometimes wish I could be a fly on the wall in the customer services office at our local supermarket, because I can well imagine that response as they go through the week's comments cards. I once read somewhere that we should become a nuisance to our supermarkets, asking questions about their policies and practices and badgering them about issues we feel are important. After all, I reason, they take so much of my money every week it would be rude not to give something back in return!

So I try to let them know my concerns at every possible opportunity. Mostly that is through the comments cards that are available at the customer services desk. I don't use them every week, but, if I read something that I would like to ask them about, or see something that worries me, then I take two or three minutes to fill in one of the forms. The nature of your reply will depend on the nature of the supermarket: whether it is positive or negative, open or defensive. More often than not, the reply will lead to my writing my own reply, and soon a regular exchange over a particular issue is happening. This often leads to the query being passed on to Head Office, who deal with it directly.

Mostly I feel like I'm banging my head against a brick wall – but not all the time. I have had some successes, most notably getting a particular fair-trade item stocked. It might just have been coincidence, but I like to think that my letters and emails contributed to the policy change.

It is easy to think that I am all on my own doing this, but actually this is far from the truth. I had been trying, unsuccessfully, to get one of the supermarkets to stock fairtrade bananas. I had been emailing backwards and forwards, all to no avail, and had finally been told that they were not going to stock them and that's that. Later, I was having a drink with a friend from another part of the country and she mentioned how she had been writing to them too about fairtrade bananas. How encouraging! Who knows? Perhaps two voices may make more impact than one.[1]

'Letters' covers a number of different methods of communication: yes, letters, but also emails, phone calls and postcards. Postcards, in particular, have become increasingly popular, with all the main campaigning charities using them as their chief weapon. These organizations recognize that many of us are just too busy to write a proper letter. A postcard with the text already on it, which we can simply sign and send, is an ideal way to motivate people to do something and to get the message across that people care about the issue at hand. And postcards are proving to be remarkably effective. The Secretary of Trade and Industry was deluged with 35,000 cards before she went to a World Trade Organization summit in November 2001, and she was unable to ignore the strength of feeling behind that number. In 1999, 30,000 postcards were sent to the Government by Friends of the Earth supporters demanding a better waste strategy, and in 2003 a related campaign bore fruit in the passing of the Household Waste Recycling Bill. These actions forced the Government to change its statutory targets. Similar successes were seen when Homebase announced it would go peat-free, partly in response to a large number of emails; and also when the Countryside and Rights of Way Act was passed in 2000, again partly as a result of 250,000 pledges being delivered to No. 10.

So writing letters and sending emails and postcards really do make a difference. As the Catholic aid agency CAFOD says, 'Writing to politicians does have a big impact. It is the easiest way to gauge the level of public interest on one particular subject. The more postcards land on the desks of MPs and senior politicians, the more seriously they are going to take that subject.' In addition, sending a card with a charity's logo on it helps the lobbying work done by that particular organization as they then gain recognition and legitimacy through having public support.

Amnesty International told me of the effect letter-writing had for this man:

> I was being kept naked in an underground cell. When the first 200 letters came, the guards gave me back my clothes. The next 200 letters came and the prison officers came to see me. When the next pile of letters arrived, the director got in touch with his superior. The letters kept coming, 3,000 of them, and the President called me to his office. He showed me an enormous box of letters he had received, and said: How is it that a trade union leader like you has so many friends all over the world?[2]

Many of the big issues are, ultimately, determined by the decisions of the big companies and by governments. But these companies and governments depend on us for their support. Big businesses are constantly pressurized by the need to be producing the next dollar for their shareholders, and they need to know that there are people who care more about other people and the environment than about making more money. We demonstrate this by our actions, but that care also needs explaining in words. If I change supermarkets, the financial loss of my weekly shop really will not be felt at all. If I write and explain why I am taking my loyalty elsewhere, however, and if they hear of others doing the same, they will begin to take notice. It is good to remember, also, to write to companies that we think are good and encourage them along the road they are taking.

Letters *are* the most effective form of communication, because they are personal and because they take time and hence represent commitment to the issue. But they do take time! I never have that time available and so I have had to make it. It can be a good idea to set aside one evening every other month, or every three months, to be your 'letter-writing evening'. Over those months you can collect together all the campaign ideas you will receive from various organizations and then, on that evening, sit down and work through them all, doing all the letters at one hit. It is easy to let it slip, so make that evening sacred!

Let us look at an example of what we could do. Let's say we are concerned about the way tropical rainforests are being destroyed to produce wood used in the furniture and paper industries. Alongside reducing our use of wood-based prod-ucts, there is letter-writing that we can do too. We can put pressure on our DIY stores and other shops to make sure all their wood products are certified by the Forest Stewardship Council, which guarantees that the wood in products bearing its logo is taken from a sustainable source. (Many of the supermarkets' wooden utensils, for example, are FSC-certified.) We can write to our daily newspaper and ask them to increase their recycled content so that less wood pulp is needed to produce paper. We can ask our local council to provide a wood recycling scheme. Finally, we can write to those banks and organizations that are directly involved in logging and farming activities that are destroying forests.[3]

Getting involved in this kind of campaigning work is all part of being an advocate: speaking up on behalf of those who cannot speak for themselves (Prov. 31:8–9). It is an integral part of 'spending ourselves on behalf of the hungry and satisfying the needs of the oppressed', and it works alongside the kind of lifestyle changes that we have been looking at so far. It is important and necessary work that is more than worth the time it takes to put our finger to the keyboard.

Action points

- Get out your diary and put in four letter-writing evenings for the next year.

- Look back over the issues tackled by the book so far and choose two topics that are of particular concern to you. Contact the relevant organizations and begin to get involved in their campaigns. Many organizations allow you to subscribe to email newsletters. These can be a very handy way of keeping in touch with key developments and concerns.

M is for Money [1]

I ran a seminar recently on the subject of 'Discipleship and money' at a large gathering of Christians from all over the UK. I led the seminar jointly with a fairly dour businessman, dressed in a suit. My word! I have never heard someone speak so passionately on the subject of money – about the excitement of having a radical attitude of detachment from money and the effects that has on our lives. At one point he even broke down in tears! Has anything so exciting ever been talked about in your church?

It is a happy coincidence that the two central letters of the alphabet give us, in this book, the two topics of money and consumerism ('N is for Needs'). Truly these two things are what make our world go round today. Money, in particular, is so often at the centre of our lives; it can form who we are, how others think of us and what we are able to do. We have touched on some things that are relevant already. In 'G is for Globalization' we got a glimpse of how our global economic system works, and in 'I is for Investments' we began to unpack some of the implications that this carries for how we conduct our own financial business.

In this book we are looking at how we can be Christian activists, spending ourselves on behalf of the hungry and considering how our lifestyles play a part in that. So many of the issues involved with this revolve around our understanding of money and possessions. That understanding can be easily moulded by the culture in which we live; but, as followers of Jesus, we want our understanding to be based on him and on the rest of God's revelation in the Bible.

In 'C is for Creation' we saw how God created the world – and created it *good*. It is a totally positive account of creation: no repudiation of the material world, but a thorough embracing of it. The fall, however, placed curses on the blessings and fullness that were there for people to enjoy.

Throughout the Old Testament there appear two strands regarding money and possessions. On the one hand, there is nothing intrinsically wrong with having either, and, indeed, some parts of the Old Testament see them as part of the promises of Yahweh for those who live according to his ways (e.g. Lev. 26:3–5; Deut. 28:1–14). God is seen as a God of tremendous blessing and generosity: a God who rescued his people *out* of poverty, rather than calling them *into* it! Wealth creation is a positive calling that God gives people, and to be denied that ability can be a denial of God's purposes for our lives (e.g. the story of Joseph in Gen. 39:2–6, and Prov. 3:9–10). We have been placed in a world full of plenty, and our response to that should not be to reject that plenty, but rather to steward it effectively.

On the other hand, wealth is not necessarily to be seen as a reward for covenant faithfulness, and other voices in the Old Testament warn of its dangers (as is evident in the lives of many of the kings, who 'did evil in the eyes of the LORD'). It is worth noting, too, that material blessing as a necessary reward from Yahweh is one strand of teaching that does *not* carry through into the New Testament.[2] In particular, the Old Testament makes it clear that a person's money or property should never be gained at the expense of another, who is thereby left in a poorer state. The prophets provide us with a strong denunciation of the gross inequality that arose within Israel (e.g. Ezek. 22:29; Amos 8:4–6).

When we turn to look at Jesus we shall be disappointed if we hope to find him concerned only with individual piety. The facts that giving is as important to him as praying and fasting (Matt. 6), and that he talks more about money than about anything else apart from the kingdom of God, demonstrate how crucial this issue was to him. He was very clear that we cannot serve both God and Mammon/Money (Matt. 6:24) and taught strongly about the dangers of money. He described riches as a strangler and as a worry (Luke 8:14; 12:22–34). Money can blind us to the eternal realities of life, and can indeed be a curse for us (Luke 16:19–31; 6:20, 24).[3]

More positively, Jesus gives us the flip-side to why we should not be preoccupied with money: because we should *seek first* the kingdom of God (Matt. 6:33). In a wonderful passage, Jesus challenges head-on our society's obsession with material things (our 'treasures') and instead puts before us the values of the kingdom (Matt. 6:19–34).[4]

Jesus' message of radical kingdom economics is summed up in two incidents in his life. First, in Luke 19:1–9, Zacchaeus shows us a person who, before meeting Jesus, put all his trust and value in his wealth. Martin Luther once said, 'Every person needs two conversions: one of the heart and one of the wallet', and here we see a person demonstrating these two conversions working together. Zacchaeus' money was earned at the expense of the poor people of Jericho and he knew that the only appropriate response on meeting Jesus was to give back all that money – four times over! As he gave away half of his possessions to the poor and then paid people back four times, we can only guess at the financial effects that had on him. It is unlikely he would have been rich after that. Here was no giving away of his surplus in order to feel better; this was a radical outworking of the Jubilee principle.

The second incident in Jesus' life was his observation of the widow who gave her two very small copper coins (Luke 21:1–4). In contrast to all the wealthy people who were also putting their gifts into the temple treasury, Jesus recognized that 'this poor widow has put in more than all the others'. Again, we see how different the values of the kingdom are from the values of society. In our world, it is size and numbers that count; we are praised for the amount we give. In Jesus' eyes, what matters is how much we have left afterwards and the sacrifice that we have been prepared to make.

The early church continued Jesus' economic ethic, as the pictures given in the early chapters of Acts bear out. What is envisaged here is not communal living with the abolition of private property – clearly, people throughout the early years of the church owned their own houses and fields – but a community that put others' needs before their own and where members were prepared to give of their own possessions and money in order to see others' needs met. The call was both to share God's blessings with his followers and not to neglect the poor with whom they came into contact.

Paul uses the collection for the church in Jerusalem as an opportunity to demonstrate that Christians' attitude towards money, and their use of it, is not a peripheral issue. In his letters we get a glimpse of the early church reaching more into the middle and upper classes.

In particular, the church at Corinth ran into problems when people expected to be able to use their wealth to buy power within the church. Paul again sets out the contrast between Jesus' way and the world's way. James, more famously, picks this up and his words contain a strong challenge for us today. Do we treat people differently according to their financial status? How does our faith outwork itself? (See also 1 John 3:17.)

What does all this mean for us today? It means that we may well need to make some changes in our attitude towards money and possessions. We shall look at this more broadly in our next chapter, but it just needs stating that the biblical position is so far removed from what our culture tells us that we need continually to check ourselves and see in which camp we stand. Of particular note here is how far we are willing even to talk about the subject. A Joseph Rowntree Foundation survey found that 95% of those surveyed thought it offensive to be questioned on how they spent their money and whether the choices they were making could be improved on. Would you have put yourself in that 95%?

Discussing my finances is certainly something I can get prickly about. Nevertheless, I have two good friends who know all about my financial situation. The three of us have sat down and gone through our budgets with one another: our monthly expenditures and incomes; our savings; our mortgages; our pensions – everything has been laid out on the table and opened to one another for questioning. As a family we are trying, slowly, to bring our financial practices and attitudes more into line with what we see in the Bible. We are far, far away from the ideal and shall be working on this for the rest of our lives, but the best way we can do it is with friends around us who will question and support any decisions we make.

Edgar Hoover said, 'A budget tells your money where to go, otherwise you wonder where it went.' On a practical level, one of the best things we can do is sort out our finances so that we know exactly how much money we have, what we spend, what we save and what we give away. When we do that we can begin to see where there might be areas of weakness that we can work on and where we might have money that we can use to help others.

This is exciting stuff! I know of one couple with a good income who live very simply. At the end of each financial year they look at what they have earned and what they have spent and they give the surplus away. Last year they gave away £30,000. For others of us it might be a question of putting a small amount of money aside each month and then giving that away when it has reached a fair amount. Perhaps we might impose on ourselves a 'luxury tax' whereby whenever we buy something that is a luxury (a bar of chocolate, cinema ticket, even a car) we buy two and give one away, or give away the equivalent sum of money.[5]

Whatever we do, our aim is to discipline our attitude towards money and our use of it to bring it into line with the Bible's teaching, so that we might use as much of our money as possible to be a blessing to others.

Action points
- If you do not already do so, work out a budget so that you know exactly what your money is doing (Credit Action can help on this – see below).

- Get together with a friend who is a mature Christian and show him or her your budget. Ask your friend to comment and advise.

- Take one step that will help you use your money more for the benefit of others. When you have done that, take another step!

Good contacts
Credit Action: 6 Regent Terrace, Cambridge CB2 1AA; 01223 324034; <www.creditaction.com>
Stewardship Services: PO Box 99, Loughton, Essex IG10 3QJ; 0208 502 5600; <www.stewardship.org.uk>

Good books
C. Blomberg, *Neither Poverty nor Riches: A Biblical Theology of Money and Possessions*
R. Sider, *Rich Christians in an Age of Hunger*

N is for Needs

A friend of mine came round to see me recently. As she walked in I absentmindedly looked down at her shoes. Instant reaction: 'Oh, don't look!' she exclaimed. 'I bought them over the weekend and I have so many pairs already. I knew I shouldn't, but once I'd seen them I couldn't put them out of my mind till I'd got them.'

Finally she admitted, 'Ruth, I think I've got a problem. I can't stop buying things. Even when I know I shouldn't, I just give in. I've got no control over myself and I need to get it sorted.'

My friend's confessions are nothing astounding and would be echoed by countless millions around the world – and probably by many of us reading this book. Gandhi once said, 'There is enough in the world for man's needs, but not for man's greed.' This encapsulates the subject of this chapter: consumerism. For consumerism has taught us to blur the edges between what is a need and what is, if we are honest, just a greed.[1]

Consumerism has been specifically cultivated over recent decades. To put it at its simplest, it is the culture whereby our primary activity and focus is consuming things, rather than producing them.

In the post-war years there was an era of mass consumption on an unprecedented scale as a productivity boom led to a capacity to supply goods and services that far outstripped demand. The only way to deal with this was to stimulate that demand: in other words, to produce a desire to consume. This led to all the marketing ploys with which we are now so familiar: advertising, built-in obsolescence, the promotion of credit cards and the opening up of new markets such as the teenagers – and now the 'tweenagers' – and the high-earning young professional market. I gave a talk recently on consumerism at which I called out various advertising slogans, and wasn't surprised to find that most people there knew the products that went with them; the ad man has done his job well!

This in itself is not necessarily a negative thing. As we saw in 'G is for Globalization', we benefit from a wonderful freedom of consumer choice, and our consumption of goods can be a blessing that allows our needs to be met.[2] The danger, though, is that as we consume, so we ourselves are consumed by the ideology of consumerism that overtakes us.

The result is that consumerism has now become the dominant force in our society and, as such, it carries with it some very powerful values. A person's identity and significance are defined by what he or she consumes, whether a house, a car, a holiday, a hair product, clothes or whatever. The advertisements all around us, particularly on the television, ensure that we know the difference between the driver of a Volvo and the driver of a New Fiesta, or a Hamlet smoker and a Bacardi drinker. Thus goods are valued for what they mean as much as for their use.

In the past, individuals' identity was bound up with their family, their faith, their values and their location. Now, identity is primarily found in what we consume and often a person will build their supporting community around their consumption habits. If you don't believe that, think of your family and friends and ask yourself to what extent your bonding with them is deepened around the things you consume (such as dinner out, a shopping trip). How much of your conversation is about activities or objects of consumption?[3]

The consumer culture is profoundly individualistic and self-centred. In this way it is closely identified with post-modernity, which stresses the autonomy of the individual and individuals' rights to have whatever they want and to be whatever they want. After all, the customer is always right.

Holding pride of place is money. Without it one cannot consume, and so money is endlessly presented as having the ability to bring status, power, freedom and hence that elusive prize: happiness. Indeed, happiness is what it's all about. Consumerism is, at its heart, the ultimate pursuit of happiness and fulfilment. It offers us a life in which nothing goes wrong. The road is always empty, the dish is always full, the colours are always bright, the clothes are always white, the hair is always perfect and the man nearly so.

We may laugh at this, but the reality is that consumerism has come at a price and has affected the most important areas of our lives. We approach our relationships through our consumer lenses. We try our relationships on for size to see if they meet our expectations and fulfil our needs. If they don't, we simply put them back on the shelf and try others. Our relationships suffer as we have to work increasingly longer hours in order to keep up with the pressure that is on us to consume more and more.

Religion, too, has succumbed to consumerism. People shop around to find the religion, or church, that fits them best. Commitment is at an all-time low: if it doesn't suit our needs we move on somewhere else. Consumerism affects our faith, and the danger for us is that we develop a compartmentalized Christianity that makes no connection between our faith on a Sunday morning and how we spend our money the rest of the week.[4] Tom Wright talks about the danger of Christianity in our society becoming 'simply a warmth-in-the-heart religion instead of a kingdom-on-earth-as-it-is-in-heaven religion'. He warns of a Christianity that becomes 'focused on me and my survival, my sense of God, my spirituality, rather than outwards on God, and on God's world that still needs the kingdom-message so badly'.[5]

The global picture of consumerism is of a world struggling to meet the demand for more, more, more. The fashion designer Katharine Hamnett teamed up with Cred a few years back to produce a teeshirt bearing the words, 'How you spend controls what happens on the planet.' There are many causes of poverty: sinful personal choices, disasters, lack of technology, western colonialism, corruption and so on, but we have to recognize that our consumerism is a part of the unjust structures that contribute to world poverty.

The positive side is that we do have a choice as to how we live our lives and how we spend our money. Taking on board earlier chapters, we see that we can not only cut down our consumption, but that we also have the power to consume in a way that actually helps to alleviate poverty.

In 'M is for Money' we looked in depth at what the Bible teaches about money and possessions, all of which is, of course, relevant here too. What else does the Bible say that speaks into our culture? In the Old Testament a good law to remember is that of keeping the Sabbath. This laid down important principles regarding rest and trusting God. It speaks to our culture of incessant work, reminding us that our work is not the be-all and end-all and that *we* are not the be-all and end-all. It confirms that, rather than economic achievement, our relationship with God, with one another and with our world is at the heart of what it means to be human and, hence, is our ultimate destiny.

Matthew 6 is a passage that speaks directly to our situation. Here, the gauntlet is thrown down. What do we put our security in? Is it in God's provision or in our material possessions? Which is more important to us? What are we investing in for the long term? Do we have an eternal perspective when we consider these things? How important are clothes and food to us? Do we 'run after these things' rather than the kingdom of God?

An overriding biblical theme that is so important for us to recover today is that of contentment. Consumerism makes us think that we need more and more and creates a continual dissatisfaction that is temporarily expunged by a trip to the shops. Its message is that we are not rich enough, beautiful enough or smart enough. In direct opposition to these messages, the voices of the Bible tell us to be content: 'Keep your lives free from the love of money and be content with what you have' (Heb. 13:5; see also Phil. 4:11-12 and 1 Tim. 6:6-10). Contentment comes from being secure in the knowledge that money and possessions are not the focus of our lives: that honour belongs to Jesus.

In Philippians 4:11-12, Paul talks of being content whatever the circumstances: not just knowing when to say that we have enough, but being content even when things are hard. A positive understanding of suffering is relevant here, since we are bombarded with messages that tell us that it is our right to be healthy and wealthy and beautiful and that personal fulfilment is based on these things. The reality of the Christian life is that Jesus promises no such thing. In fact, the Bible represents the life of faith as a generally hard, unrewarding and even painful experience and Jesus speaks of it as a cross. Rather than expecting to experience a carefree life with no suffering, Christians can expect instead to find the grace and strength to go through these difficulties knowing that, ultimately, they are victorious in Christ.

Romans 12:1-2 urges: 'Do not conform any longer to the pattern of this world, but be transformed by the renewing of your mind.' Nowhere is this more germane than in this chapter. Describing the culture of consumerism as Boom City, Tom and Christine Sine write:

> What has happened is that we haven't just moved into Boom City, Boom City has moved into us. More than we recognize, Boom City has branded us and defined, even for people of vital faith, what is important and what is of value. We have unwittingly allowed Boom City to write the mission statement for our lives and families, but few of us seemed to notice.

They go on to say:

> We shall only find God's best when we refuse to conform any longer to the aspirations and values of Boom City and invite God to transform our inmost sense of what is important and of value which will in turn change the direction and tempo of our lives.[6]

As followers of Jesus we live by a story different from that told by our culture. We know that we do not need to be surrounded by 'stuff' in order to find fulfilment. As we simplify our lives and refuse to be shackled by the chains of consumerism, we shall discover a new sense of joy and liberation.

Action points[7]

- Don't watch television for a week, month or year. Then ask yourself: how did I feel about it? Did I miss it? What happened instead?

- Sort through your clothing, kitchen cupboards or even your whole house (!) and box up anything that you don't need or use. If, after three months, you have not opened the box at all, give its contents away.

- When you go shopping, take this list of questions with you:
  - ☐ Do I really need this product? Why?
  - ☐ Is this an impulsive purchase or have I planned it?
  - ☐ Have I done research to find the best product to meet my needs?
  - ☐ Do I know the environmental consequences of this purchase?
  - ☐ Does this product meet fair-trade standards?
  - ☐ Can I borrow it? Share it with someone? Buy it second hand?
  - ☐ Was it made or grown locally, perhaps saving energy and packing?

Good books
T. and C. Sine, *Living on Purpose*
B. Rosner, *How to Get Really Rich*

O is for Organic

'Didn't we do this already in "F is for Food?"' I hear you ask? In our chapter on Food we did begin to look at the reasons for buying and eating more organic produce. We looked there at the heavy use of pesticides that is part of most modern methods of farming and the damage that this is causing to the land, to the wider environment, to our wildlife, to our farmed animals and to our health. There is more to consider, though, and I want to look further at organic food in this chapter, as well as move it beyond just this issue alone.

The one factor that always comes up alongside the subject of organic food is price, as there is no doubt that, by and large, organic produce is more expensive than non-organic.[1] Why is this the case?[2] We need to ask ourselves, first, why non-organic food is so cheap. One reason is farming subsidies. These subsidies are calculated by the number of animals per hectare and the size of the cropped area: the higher the number the more help the farmer receives. This inevitably favours intensive, non-organic farming.

The second reason is that the external costs that the intensive farmer creates is paid for by the taxpayer. These costs include those of cleaning up rivers contaminated by chemicals (which is then reflected in our water bills), repairing wildlife habitats, and coping with sickness and disasters caused by farming (such as BSE – which cost the British taxpayer £4 billion – and Foot and Mouth).

All these things are paid for by our taxes. It is estimated that an average family of four in the EU spends £16 a week on agricultural subsidies, on top of their food bills. Likewise, they spend an extra £11 a week on clean-up costs.

The third reason it is so cheap is that cheapness is what we expect and demand. It is interesting to see that, over the last thirty years, the percentage of our household budget spent on food has dropped, on average, from 24% to 16%. We then choose to spend that money on other items. In 1998, the average household spent almost the same amount on food and non-alcoholic drinks as they did on leisure goods and services. Quantity, rather than quality, is thus what we have been given. While our supermarket bill may make the food look cheap, however, it begins to look less cheap when we consider the hidden costs that the taxpayer is having to cover.

In this way we are paying for our food three times: once over the counter, the second time in subsidies and the third in clean-up costs.

Having considered the cost of cheap food, we then need to look at what goes into organic farming. To put it at its simplest, organic food is more expensive because it is more labour-intensive to farm without chemicals; the yields are often lower, and parts of the farm lie fallow each year to increase fertility and so cannot generate an income. The conversion process, particularly, can be an expensive time; the farmer cannot charge the premium price for organic produce, yet the yields will be lower and the initial expenses higher. What results from this process, however, is farms that practise a high standard of animal welfare, with crop rotation, strong environmental practices and the use of skilled techniques rather than a dependency on chemicals.

101

The cost of buying organic can be a bitter pill to swallow for those of us wanting to support its development. When you consider the illusion involved in our so-called cheap food and then look at what goes into organic farming, however, there can be no doubt that organic food is definitely worth the extra.

So far, we have been concentrating on organic food. But many people are now beginning to realize that being organic reaches beyond just that one issue. Around 250 million tonnes of 80,000 different chemicals are produced every year and are used in everything we meet: sofas, computers, TVs, detergents, paints, mattresses, toys, windows, tins, and so on. There is no doubt that the chemical industry contributes to our quality of life and we could not live the life we do without the use of many of these chemicals. The European Commission, however, states that only a proportion of chemicals used has been fully tested, and the evidence is increasing that some of them are damaging our health, leading to a whole host of problems, from earlier puberty to allergies.[3] The recent drive towards organic is about reducing our exposure to these chemicals, and this reaches into every area of our lives. Here are three of the most important.

If organic food is a concern, the next logical step is to extend that into our *gardening* practices. After all, there is little point supporting organic developments if you scatter slug pellets over your flowerbeds and douse your plants in insecticide! Gardening brings some of the most satisfying pleasures of life. What better way to garden than in a way that enhances the small ecosystem you have charge over; encouraging birds, bees and butterflies and providing space for local wildlife?[4]

A very important area to consider is *cleaning products*. These are all stuffed full of chemicals, some of them very harmful, both to the environment and to our health. Thankfully, there are now very good, environmentally friendly products, readily available in supermarkets and health food shops.[5] When we know about the damaging effects of regular cleaners, how can we not use these products instead? As always, they can be slightly more expensive. If this is a particular concern for you, consider going back to basics and making your own cleaning solutions: bicarbonate of soda, for example, does an amazing job.[6]

A third area that is growing slowly in the public's consciousness is that of the *beauty products* many of us use. It has been estimated that a woman can absorb up to 2 kg of chemicals a year through the products she uses on her skin.[7] Many skincare products are used twice a day. Generally we have no idea what has gone into them and there is little regulation around that. Sodium laureth sulphate, for example, is the second-biggest ingredient in most shampoos, shower gels and bubble baths, but is surrounded by controversy over possible negative effects. I am beginning to realize that, if I don't want to eat chemicals, I also don't want to put them on my skin. As with cleaning, so also with beauty products: there are alternatives to buy and recipes to make, and great fun can be had finding out about them and experimenting.[8]

Becoming more organic is part of developing a lifestyle that takes more care of ourselves and of the world that God has made. The Old Testament makes it clear that respect for the land that God has given us is an integral part of our relationship with God and with one another (see 'C is for Creation'). The encouraging news is that, as Michael Van Straten says, every step does make a difference:

> Every family that encourages a household culture of organic living makes an even greater difference, by educating their children to live organically in the future. Every tiny saving of fuel and every purchase of organic food will help. Each of these small steps contributes to a reduction of toxic material in our environment and a lower rate of global warming.[9]

Action points

- Find out more about the issues around organics by contacting the organizations involved in its promotion, such as the Soil Association and the Henry Doubleday Research Association (HDRA).

- Choose one food product, one cleaning product and one beauty product and change them to organic.

Good contacts

Friends of the Earth 'Safer Chemicals' campaign (see 'C is for Creation')
Henry Doubleday Research Association (HDRA): Ryton Organic Gardens, Ryton on Dunsmore, Coventry CV8 3LG:

02476 303517; <enquiry@hdra.org.uk>;
<www.hdra.org.uk>
The Soil Association (see 'F is for Food')

A good book
M. Van Straten, *Organic Living*

P is for Paper[1]

As I sit at my desk I am surrounded by paper wherever I look. I use paper constantly through my day. The postman brings me letters; I write the milkman a note, scribble down a shopping list, print out a map for a speaking engagement ... I am not alone in this. In fact, Britain is the fifth-highest paper-user in the world, despite its size.[2]

Our demand for paper is one of the key factors behind deforestation, which, in turn, is the second-highest contributor to climate change, only behind burning fossil fuels. Deforestation contributes to climate change through the carbon the trees absorb through photosynthesis: scientists describe rainforests as 'carbon sinks'. Thus they are one of the main ways in which carbon (in the form of carbon dioxide) is absorbed out of the atmosphere. Because they absorb so much, when forests are felled and burned the carbon dioxide is released back into the atmosphere (as also are nitrous oxide and ozone). In this way, deforestation is responsible for 20-30% of all carbon dioxide in the atmosphere.

Tropical rainforests are not the only type of forest in the world: there are also temperate forests (in northern Russia, North America, Chile and Australia), boreal forests (in the cold north of Europe and North America) and temperate rainforests (on the west coast of North America).[3] All of these contain huge varieties of wildlife and all are increasingly under threat from our demand for timber and the resources these forests hold. It is the tropical rainforests, however, that are particularly significant.

Tropical rainforests are the Earth's oldest living eco-systems: forests in South-east Asia have existed for 70-100 million years. While they cover a relatively small amount of land area, they house half of all the plant and animal species in the world. Still, scientists estimate that there could be as many as 30,000 plant species yet to be discovered.

They are incredibly rich in both medicinal substances and foodstuffs. A quarter of the medicines we use today come from rainforest plants and they have been indispensable in treating leukaemia, Hodgkin's disease, heart ailments, hyper-tension and arthritis, as well as being used in birth control. Even so, again, less than 1% of tropical plants have been examined thoroughly for their chemical compounds. It is thought that cures for cancer and Aids may well be found in there.

Much of our food originated in the rainforests, including bananas, avocados, various nuts, chocolate, rice, tomatoes, cloves and corn (the full list is much longer). While all of these are now being produced away from the rainforests, the genetic material from the wild strains is needed to keep the modern stock strong and healthy.

While they may be far away, therefore, the rainforests are hugely important to us and are rich in resources. And yet they are facing intense pressure. All the primary (i.e. original) rainforests in India, Bangladesh, Sri Lanka and Haiti have been destroyed. Every second 2.4 acres is destroyed; 149 acres every minute; 214,000 acres each day (an area larger than New York City) and 78 million acres each year (an area larger than Poland). The rainforests of the Ivory Coast have almost been completely destroyed. The Philippines lost 55% of its forests between 1960 and 1985 and, by 1985, Thailand had lost 45%.

Why is this happening? There are six main causes of deforestation, all of which relate to what we saw in 'E is for Energy' regarding human greed and selfishness. This demonstrates again how the environmental crisis is, fundamentally, a spiritual issue.

First, the most obvious cause is logging, due to the world's demand for wooden and paper goods. Take a moment to think through all the rooms in your house. How much of the contents are made from wood?

The second cause is farming: primarily to produce beef for richer countries, particularly in fast-food outlets and processed products. In 1993 and 1994, America imported over 91 million kg of fresh and frozen beef from Central American countries. Whether the forest is cleared for cattle-grazing or for crop-farming, the thin rainforest soil grows pasture for only a few years, and then cattle-ranchers and farmers are forced to move on, cutting down yet more forest.

Thirdly, the rainforests are being increasingly mined for minerals such as aluminium and tin.

Fourthly, oil extraction threatens large areas. BP, Chevron, Shell, Exxon, Conoco Inc. and Occidental are all involved in 'exploring' different rainforest areas. The extraction leads to massive degradation and pollution, as well as affecting human rights as tribal territories are invaded.

Fifthly, in order for any of this work to happen, roads are needed for access and electricity is needed for power, and so hydroelectric dams are being built that flood big areas of forest and displace the people that lived there. It should be noted here that all of this depends on the companies' having enormous amounts of money, and the World Bank and some of our High Street banks are involved in providing the necessary capital.

Finally, subsistence farming creates problems as poor farmers are forced to burn down areas of forest in order to grow crops to eat and sell. As with HIV/Aids, so deforestation also is clearly linked with issues of poverty, as the uneven distribution of land and money plays a part here. There is a direct link between deforestation and the global structures that we have noted earlier in this book. One example is Brazil, where international debt is repaid primarily through exporting cash crops. This leads to the inevitable clear-cutting of the forests to provide the land on which to grow the cash crops.[4]

It won't be a surprise to hear that deforestation is causing enormous problems, not least to the indigenous people themselves who have lived in the forests for thousands of years. Many tribes have lost their homelands and have been intimidated and murdered when they have tried to resist this happening. In Brazil, in 1500, 6–9 million people lived in the rainforests. Now there are fewer than 200,000. As tribes disappear, do we lose something of the colour and variety that form the 'great multitude' worshipping before God's throne (Rev. 7:9)? It is a sad reality too that, all too often, poverty and disenfranchisement result from people's losing their homeland. It is interesting to note that an acre of rainforest land is thought to be over six times more financially lucrative if sustainably harvested for fruits, latex and timber than if clear-cut for commercial timber.

The environmental damage caused by deforestation extends beyond climate change. We saw in 'E is for Energy' the spiritual nature of species extinction, and deforestation is causing the loss of biodiversity that is resulting in an alarming rate of species extinction. It is thought that 10% of the world's species could disappear within twenty-five years because of the breakdown of rainforest ecosystems. Remembering what we saw earlier about medicine and food, this has implications for us too.

Is there anything we can do into this situation? As with much of what we have seen already, the stakes are high and the other players powerful. There is much money to be made out of the rainforests, and vested interests do not give up those interests easily. Nevertheless, there are still actions that we can, and must, take if we are to stop these hugely precious areas of forest being destroyed.

While there are a number of different steps we could focus on (such as reducing our beef consumption from fast-food outlets and in processed foods), the most important priority is to cut down our use of paper and wood. Particularly with regard to paper, this is something that I have been working on, and now use almost no new paper at all. I re-use everything before it finally goes in the recycling box, including envelopes (particularly the postage-paid ones that we can legitimately use for our own use). I keep letters I have been sent if the paper is in good condition and I don't mind others seeing them, and then use the other side for my own letters. I finish the letters by saying, 'Please forgive the informality of re-using paper for this letter' and, so far, I've had no complaints!

Then, we must ensure that, when we do buy new paper or wood products, they come from 'sound' sources. Any wood you buy *must* have the FSC (Forest Stewardship Council) certificate on it if you are to be sure that it is not involved in deforestation. Be wary of labels saying that the wood comes from a 'sustainable source', and take the time and trouble to find out what this really means. This may be the case, but often old-growth forests (for instance, in Canada or Sweden) have been cut down in order to provide the ground. The new forests are often really just tree factories that cannot support the wildlife that existed in the original forests.[5] By buying from these sources we are encouraging this to happen more.

Any paper you buy (including toilet paper and kitchen paper) should have the highest percentage of recycled content possible: post-consumer recycled content is best. You can buy paper products, as well as wood, that are certified by the FSC. By cutting down our usage, rather than cutting down trees, we shall know that we are doing our bit to help save these amazing parts of our world.

109

Action points
- Look at your use of paper. What steps can you take to reduce the amount you use?

- Vast amounts of paper are wasted through junk mail. Whenever you get something through the post, use their reply-paid envelope to ask them to remove you from their mailing list. The Mailing Preference Service will take your name off all mailing lists (except those of companies with which you already have a relationship). Write to them at FREEPOST 22, London W1E 7EZ, or register on the website: <www.tpsonline.org.uk>.

- Don't buy fast food unless you can guarantee the meat wasn't raised in the rainforests. If you have children who are magnetically drawn to the outlets, take some time to explain to them why you would rather not eat there.[6]

Good contacts
Forest Stewardship Council: Unit D, Station Buildings, Llanidloes, Powys SY18 6EB; 01686 413916; <www.fsc-uk.info>; <info@fsc-uk.org>

Friends of the Earth (see 'C is for Creation')
Rainforest Action Network: <www.ran.org>
Woodland Trust: FREEPOST, Autumn Park, Grantham, Lincs
NG31 6BR; 01476 581136; <www.woodland-trust.org.uk>

110   R is for Recyling[1]

I went on holiday once to Indonesia, visiting my brother, who was living there. We had a wonderful time travelling across the Indonesian islands. One of my most vivid memories was crossing from one island to another on a large local boat. There were quite a few bins, which people diligently used. As we drew near to the shore, I leaned over the side of the boat to take in the view: stunning white beach, clear blue coralled sea, coconut palms lining the beach – and watched as, to my horror, the crew took all the bins and one by one tipped their contents into the sea!

Waste is a problem that is facing all of us, wherever we live in the world. Those of us living in the richer nations might like to think that we are too sophisticated to tip our rubbish into the sea so blatantly, but the fact remains that, in the UK, we throw away 165 million tonnes of waste every year.[2] Indeed, our waste is increasing: from 397 kg per person per year in 1983/4 to 498 kg per person in 1999/2000; a rise of almost 26%.[3] Like the Indonesian boatmen, we can easily think that, once we have thrown our rubbish away, it has disappeared and we need no longer think about it. But this couldn't be further from the truth.

Just under 90% of our rubbish is buried in landfill tips. As the rubbish biodegrades it produces carbon dioxide and methane (a greenhouse gas 200 times as powerful as carbon dioxide), contributing to climate change. It also produces a toxic 'leachate' that seeps into groundwater.[4] In 1998, research showed that babies born within 3 km of toxic landfill sites, and potentially all landfills, were more likely to suffer birth defects than babies born elsewhere.[5] In addition, landfill sites can give rise to problems such as increased traffic, noise, odours, smoke, dust, litter and pests.

Throwing so much away puts untold pressure on the Earth's resources. Everything we use has to have come from somewhere and has to have been made from something, whether oil for plastics; sand, soda ash and limestone for glass; raw materials and minerals for steel and aluminium; or wood for paper and cardboard. As we have seen elsewhere, many of these materials are obtained in ways that damage the rest of creation, and often harm the people who live nearby.

The harsh reality, also, is that we are running out of landfill sites. In the search for alternatives, the authorities often turn to incineration as a solution. Those bodies promoting incinerators point to the fact that the energy they produce can be harnessed positively. The energy produced, however, is far less than the energy that is saved by recycling. Incineration, therefore, destroys valuable resources and leads to the use of more fossil-fuel energy in order to replace the products. It also undermines councils' recycling schemes, which demand a constant supply of waste in order to be economic. Some councils have even had to bring in waste from other areas and abandon their plans for waste reduction and recycling.

Incineration is also polluting. It produces emissions of

particulates, heavy metals and dioxins, which are potentially dangerous to our health, and produces toxic ash, which then still has to be landfilled. Incineration does not even afford an employment opportunity, as it offers very few jobs compared with those offered by recycling. Overall, incineration is more costly than recycling and, as with landfill sites, noise and traffic become a problem.

No; the best solution is found in the three R's that have become the mantra of the environmental world: Reduce, Re-use, Recycle.

Reduce

E. F. Schumacher said, 'We tolerate a high rate of waste and then try to cope with the problem of recycling. Would it not be more intelligent first of all to try and reduce the rate of waste? The recycling problem may then itself become much more manageable.'[6] We should try, at every possible opportunity, to reduce the amount we use, and hence the amount we throw away. As a general rule, anything with the label 'disposable' should be avoided, and we should always ensure that we buy things to last.

A lot of our rubbish comes in the form of packaging. Germany has seen a 12% decrease in packaging over the last five years, whereas the packaging industry in the UK is planning for continual growth. Buying locally produced food from local outlets is often one of the best ways to reduce the packaging we buy, as supermarkets so often go overboard in this area – particularly with processed food. If you've got the nerve, try taking off all the unnecessary packaging on products that you are buying and leave it at the checkout – or, preferably, with the shop manager! What we looked at in 'N is for Need' is relevant too, since, if we are always insisting on the latest clothes and equipment, we shall inevitably produce more waste as we throw the old things out.

One little-discussed aspect here is that of sanitary protection and all the plastic and cardboard packaging that goes with that (not to mention all the potentially damaging non-organic cotton that is used for its production). In the UK, over 3 billion sanitary towels, tampons and panty liners are bought every year, most of which are flushed down the toilet. As much as 50% of beach pollution consists of used sanitary protection. Rather than flushing it down the toilet, sanitary protection should be put in the bin. In addition, there is a very good range of protection that uses the minimum of packaging and is made from organic cotton.[7]

113

The packaging we buy is only one part of the problem. As you open your eyes to this issue you may begin to notice practices of governments, councils and businesses – both locally and nationally – that go against the principle of reducing waste. Your local council recycling officer, your MP or Government Minister, and shop managers, are good people to go to voice your concerns.

Re-use

In our disposable culture it seems so much more natural to throw something away rather than to consider how we might re-use it and thus avoid wasting resources and energy to make a new product. Plastic bags are a classic example – the scourge of our society! Have a policy never to accept one, and get into the habit of always having a couple (both carrier bags and fresh-produce bags) in your bag just in case you need one unexpectedly. The supermarket plastic boxes are excellent to use. Although the initial manufacturing is harmful, they are very long-lasting and useful for all sorts of things. I use them to put my recycling in and then empty them at the recycling facilities at the supermarket before doing a shop.

The near-universal use of 'one stop' containers is another example. Containers for food, drinks, beauty products and cleaning products could all be designed to be refillable, thus cutting down on the vast amount of cans and plastic that we dispose of each time we buy more of the same item. My local wholefood store is just beginning to introduce a refillable scheme for Ecover cleaning products. In Denmark, all drinks must be sold in returnable, glass containers.

If we have young children, an area where we can make a vast difference is in using re-usable nappies. Currently, disposable nappies account for 4% of landfill and is becoming one of the major waste issues. Each nappy uses a lot of energy and resources in production and then can take up to 500 years to decompose. Washing nappies really is not the hassle that parents using 'disposables' tend to think it is. I know of friends using 'disposables' who do much more washing than I do! As *Go M.A.D!* says, 'Babies survived right up until the 1970s with cotton nappies. Why can't we all still use them now? They produce 60 times less solid waste than disposables. It's time to clean up our act.'[8]

Recycle

Finally, when we have reduced and re-used as much as we can, we can look to see if we can recycle (and remember to buy recycled too). Recyling is far more efficient in terms of energy and resources than landfilling or incinerating, and reduces the habitat damage caused by the extraction of raw materials. It promotes personal responsibility for the waste that we produce. It is good at job creation: for every million tonnes of waste processed, landfill creates 40-60 jobs, incineration 100-290 jobs, and recycling 400-590 jobs.[9]

Our record here in the UK, however, is dismal. Between 70% and 80% of waste could be recycled, but currently only 6.5% actually is. Almost everything we use can be recycled: our kitchen and garden waste, paper, glass, plastic, cans, foil, textiles, furniture, other household goods, batteries, wood, oil and tyres.[10] Many of these we can dispose of easily through composting, recycling bins and kerb-side collection schemes. (If your council doesn't do one, make that a priority to press for.) Other items may take more time and investigation.[11] There may yet be some waste for which there are no local facilities. If this is the case, ask your council to provide them.

All of this is our responsibility and part of how we take care of God's creation. After all, 'There is no such thing as waste in nature – the output from one organism is the input for another. As part of nature we too can take steps to make waste an irrelevant concept.'[12]

Action points

• Look at what goes into your bin. What is its highest content? Take steps to reduce that.

• Next time you go round the supermarket, make a note of all the excess packaging and unnecessary plastic and cans you see. Write a letter when you get home, or drop a note into the Customer Comments box, listing it all and asking them to adopt measures to reduce it and change their use of plastic and cans.

• Find out about the recycling facilities in your area. Are there gaps? If so, ask your council to fill them.

Good contacts
Friends of the Earth (see 'C is for Creation')
Your local council

A good book
Friends of the Earth, *Don't Throw it all Away*

S is for Simplicity[1]

Do your toes curl when you hear the word 'simplicity'? Do you think of woolly jumpers and mung-bean stew? I can't say I blame you if you do, but I hope to show you that simplicity is actually about something far more exciting.

Henry Thoreau, one of the great writers on this issue, said that 'a person is rich in proportion to the things they can leave alone' and, in many ways, this sums up what simple living is all about. Partly, it's about our choices. As we look at our lives, do we know how we've ended up living how we're living, and why? What choices have we made that control our present lifestyle? When we wanted that new house or car, were we aware that the trade-off would mean working longer hours to pay for them and seeing less of the people we love? Too often we find ourselves on the treadmill of life, paying the consequences for choices we hardly knew we were making.

Simple living is also about stopping that treadmill and giving us the space to choose how we want to live our lives. There are many voices around us that tell us that happiness is to be found in good clothes and nice jewellery; in a job that commands respect; in crashing out in front of the TV in order to recover; in having a busy diary. Simplicity asks us to sit and listen to those other whispers inside us that we seldom have the time to hear. It helps us to discover the happiness that comes, not from having an abundance of money and things, but from having the space for intimacy in our friendships, the space for ourselves and, primarily, the space for God.

Too often our days are spent thinking about the future: we drive the kids to school or drive to work while planning what we shall do that day, on autopilot, hardly noticing anything or anybody we drive past. As we talk to a friend on the phone we are thinking about what we shall have for lunch and fail to hear what she is really saying. We shove a plastic container in the microwave and eat its contents while thinking about a later meeting, and miss the pleasure of eating good, simple food.

117

Simple living is about being joyfully *aware* of what we do and why we do it. We can live in the present as well as the future, having the room to savour each moment of our lives. Above all, simple living is about getting rid of the clutter in our lives so that we can hear the voice of God more clearly and serve him more readily. As we do that, we shall discover what it really means to be rich; for simplicity is not about meanness and poverty, but about true abundance (John 10:10).

Already, from what has been said so far, it will be apparent how this subject is relevant to the theme of this book. We might say that the concept of simplicity consolidates much of what we have looked at previously. Many people are recognizing that there is something wrong with the way we live our lives. We live in an extraordinary time, with communication and technical advances developing rapidly, medical science achieving miracles and consumer choice at its highest, and yet with global inequality at an extreme. In the light of this we have to ask ourselves the question that Micah asked (see Mic. 6:8): 'What does the Lord require of me?' In our world today, what does it mean to 'act justly and to love mercy'? How do I 'walk humbly' with my God? A Christian approach to simplicity provides a helpful answer.

As we saw in 'N is for Needs', our culture today is consumer-based. It is profoundly self-centred and individualistic, placing value in the things we possess and giving prestige to those who indulge themselves in luxury and waste. We have created a short-term, throwaway culture.

It is into this context that simplicity speaks. One of the key areas is our *time*. Time is God's creation and his gift to us. He has given it to us to enjoy and to use for his service. We each have it in equal amounts, and how we choose to steward that time is our responsibility. Simple living allows time to be the most rewarding and beautiful possession that we have, helping us to reach a place of wholeness and awareness both of ourselves and of God.

And yet, 'I haven't got the time' is one of the most frequently heard complaints of our society. As a result, many of us are suffering, with stress, sleep problems and relationship pressures becoming increasingly common. What is also clear is that the situation is only going to get worse. As Tom Sine says, 'That means we shall have less time for family and friends, less time to pray and study Scripture and less time to volunteer to address the mounting needs of the poor in our societies.'[2]

One of the greatest ironies of time is that it often seems to be directly disproportional to the amount of money we have. Time is one of the greatest dividers: between those who spend time to save money and those who spend money to save time. 'The new materialism is to do with our attitude to time.'[3] Time has now become a status symbol; we measure our worth by our busyness and believe ourselves to be indispensable to all that goes on around us.

Our use of time reflects the values of our lives, and 'now' is a good time to ask ourselves whether or not we are truly living out God's values. If not, what needs to change? Many of us need to make changes so that we have the time simply to be: to be with ourselves and to be with God. Time in this sense has been described as 'opening space in our lives for a greater awareness of God'.[4]

For many, a helpful way for this to happen is through the practices of silence, solitude and contemplation.[5] Let us touch the surface by looking at Gerald May's three suggestions as to how we can begin to create space.[6]

First, he suggests looking for spaces that occur normally in our lives. Perhaps there are times that we automatically fill by turning on the TV or making ourselves a drink, but that we could make 'intentional': moments to stop and be still.

Secondly, we should try to find the more regular, set-aside spaces during the day that are 'simply and solely dedicated to just being'. However long they are, they are an opportunity to take some space and establish ourselves with Jesus at the centre.

Finally, May recommends building longer spaces into our lives for authentic retreat. These may involve actually going away for a retreat or just taking a day of quiet.

Our aim is to bring our use of time under control so that it serves our kingdom values rather than those of the world; living intentionally in each moment of time. Henri Nouwen's description of this is beautiful. He talks of a life

> ... in which time slowly loses its opaqueness and becomes
> transparent. This is often a very difficult and slow process, but full
> of re-creating power. To start seeing that the many events of our
> day, week or year are not in the way of our search for a full life, but
> the way to it, is a real experience of conversion. If we discover that
> writing letters ... visiting people and cooking food are not a series
> of random events which prevent us from realizing our deepest self,
> but contain in themselves the transforming power we are looking
> for, then we are beginning to move from time lived as chronos to
> time lived as kairos.[7]

Time is a good place to start a consideration of simplicity because it teaches us the importance of an inner simplicity, something we touched on in 'A is for Activists' where we saw the importance of prayer in our activity. As simplicity touches our approach towards money, the food we eat, the clothes we wear and so on, we remember that it begins with our heart attitude and only then moves on to our outward practice.[8]

This book is about inspiring you to 'act justly and to love mercy'. Simplicity has these things at its heart and is desperately needed today. As Richard Foster says, 'Our task is urgent and relevant. Our century thirsts for the authenticity of simplicity; the spirit of prayer, and the life of obedience. May we be the embodiment of that kind of authentic living.'[9]

Action points
- Foster has ten principles of simplicity:
    1 Buy things for their usefulness rather than their status.
    2 Reject anything that is producing an addiction in you. Learn to distinguish between a real psychological need, like cheerful surroundings, and an addiction.
    3 Develop the habit of giving things away.
    4 Refuse to be propagandized by the custodians of modern gadgetry.
    5 Learn to enjoy things without owning them.
    6 Develop a deeper appreciation for your creation.
    7 Look with a healthy scepticism at all 'buy now, pay later' schemes.
    8 Obey Jesus' instructions about plain, honest speech. 'Simply let your "Yes" be "Yes", and your "No", "No"; anything beyond this comes from the evil one' (Matt. 5:37).
    9 Reject anything that breeds the oppression of others.

10 Shun anything that distracts you from seeking first the kingdom of God.

Which of these strike you as interesting or particularly challenge you?

- How can you develop an inner simplicity?

Good contacts
Earth Ministry: <www.earthministry.org>
Simple Living Network: <www.slnet.com>

121

Good books
R. Foster, *Freedom of Simplicity*
M. Schut (ed.), *Simpler Living, Compassionate Life*
J. Odgers and R. Valerio, *Simplicity, Love and Justice*

T is for Tourism

I remember attending a tourist promotion with my husband, the sort where you are promised a free holiday if you sit through a presentation. Our poor sales rep knew he was on to a loser when he asked where we had most recently travelled to and we replied, 'Ethiopia.'

Somehow that didn't rank highly as a prime tourist destination. A few more questions later, it soon became clear that we weren't his average holidaymakers. Not very politely, he told us that we were wasting his time and might as well leave right away. We were more than happy to do so and skip the two-hour presentation – and we still got a free break in Cornwall!

Our man got no commission off us that day, but I don't think he minded really. The room was full of people signing up to the promise of wonderful holidays abroad at a price they could afford. Everyone loves going on holiday: a time to get away from it all, relax, experience something different, perhaps to enjoy some rare luxury. For many of us, our holidays are essential if we are to survive the busyness of our lives. As seen in 'G is for Globalization', one of the results of globalization is increased mobility, and we travel all over the world as tourists. As I write this I have one friend travelling through East Asia and another holidaying in India.

Strange as it may seem, most of our holidays are part of a vast industry. In fact, tourism is the biggest industry in the world.[1] There were 693 million 'tourist arrivals' in 2001, with tourists spending $463 billion around the world.[2] In the UK alone, over 36 million overseas holidays were taken in 2002 (21 million of which were package holidays) and ABTA (the Association of British Travel Agents) recorded a combined turnover of £36 billion.[3]

As with all industries, tourism can bring immense economic benefits to the countries involved: an important point when you consider that more than 30% of international tourists visit the developing world.[4] It is the number-one ranked employer in Australia, the Bahamas, Brazil, Canada, France, Germany, Italy, Jamaica and Japan, and the major source of income in Bermuda, Greece, Italy, Spain, Switzerland and most Caribbean countries.[5] Tourism is growing in, or significant to the economy of, eleven of the twelve countries that account for 80% of the world's poor.[6]

There are programmes trying to ensure that tourism

benefits the receiving countries, such as the AITO Responsible Tourism Code, the Tour Operators Initiative for Sustainable Tourism Development, and 'Sustainable Tourism – Eliminating Poverty'; an initiative owned by the WTO and UNCTAD. In the UK, ABTA is increasingly recognizing the importance of 'responsible tourism' and has been liaising with its membership, pressure groups and the UK Government over how to develop tourism sustainably.[7]

These initiatives demonstrate the presence of ethically responsible tour operators. So, for example, <responsibletravel.com> enables travellers to find a diversity of pre-screened holidays that will benefit the hosts and their environment as well as the traveller. These holidays are provided by many of the world's leading tour operators, accommodation-owners and grassroots community projects.[8]

As positive as these initiatives are, however, they are but a drop in the ocean. The necessity for such special programmes shows that tourism also has negative effects on the receiving countries, particularly in those that are less economically developed. One of the biggest problems is that, while the tourism industry can turn over a staggering figure, often a large proportion of that money stays in the tourist-sending countries. In some cases as little as 10p of every £1 spent may stay in low-income countries.[9] The tourist's demands mean that they may stay in foreign-owned hotels, eating imported food, and visiting attractions with fixed prices arranged by the hotel chain.

Another concern is that of human-rights abuses and the implicit support that a tourist is giving a government by travelling to its country. An article in *The Observer* newspaper accused tourists of turning a blind eye to rights abuses and of putting bargain holidays before ethical concerns.[10] It cited countries such as Turkey, Indonesia and the Gambia as having poor human-rights records but still attracting tourists in large numbers. In particular, the article accused British travellers of being 'among the most unethical travellers in the world, ignoring global environmental damage and riding roughshod over local populations and their needs'.

Tourism itself can also lead to human-rights abuses. For example, at the beginning of 1988, pastoralists were evicted from the Mkomazi Game Reserve in Tanzania. Some of their homes were razed to the ground and some livestock was rounded up and sold by the Government to pay for the evictions. People received no compensation and were literally left by the roadside with 40,000 cattle. The reason for this was tourism development: to meet the demand for safaris. A recent success story is that of the Nungwi peninsula in Zanzibar, which was under threat of being turned into an international resort, displacing 20,000 people. A campaign headed up by Tourism Concern stopped that happening.[11]

The bestselling book, *The Beach*, was the story of every backpacker's dream to find a place untouched by tourism's destructive hands; the irony being that it was the tourists themselves who brought that destruction. When it comes to environmental issues, tourism has a bad record. The Christian environmental organization, A Rocha, was started as a result of the effects of tourism on the Algarve coast, where mass tourism and EC grants led to the destruction of cork-oak plantations, almond and olive orchards and sustainable fishing, replacing them with the rapid (but often unsustainable) profits of hotels, golf courses and marinas.[12]

Environmental problems due to tourism are often most severe in less economically developed countries due to the tourists' demand for a standard of living way above that of the local people and an expectation of luxuries while on holiday. I well remember travelling through Rajasthan, when my brother got married in India, and staying in hotels that allowed me to shower every day, while the region was suffering a drought. Tourism Concern states that a typical tourist uses as much water in one day as a rural villager would use to produce rice for 100 days.[13] Similarly, an eighteen-hole golf course can consume as much water as a town of 10,000 people.[14]

Perhaps the biggest environmental problem facing tourism is how we get there in the first place. Cheaper flights mean that more and more of us are choosing to travel by aeroplane. It is forecast that by 2030 in the UK there will be 500 million plane passengers a year.[15] The problems are immense: climate change from the carbon dioxide emissions (air travel is the fastest-growing source of emissions), health risks from toxic nitrogen oxide emissions, noise pollution, and development pressures with road traffic congestion and with greenfield sites tarmacked over for runways and car parks.

The harsh reality is that our flying habits need to be severely curtailed, if not stopped altogether. For many of us that might not be an option, however, particularly if our work requires us to fly regularly. One option we have is to make our flights 'carbon neutral'. We can do this by contributing to a scheme that offsets our emissions by funding projects that reduce greenhouse gases, such as reforestation and renewable energies.[16]

Interestingly, MORI research shows that, given the choice, around eight out of ten British travellers would pay to offset the environmental impact of their flights, car rental or hotels (£7 per flight; £1 per one week car rental and £1 per night in a hotel). As positive a sign as this is, though, the accusation could be levelled at those of us from wealthier countries that we just use our money to offset anything. Should we not go further in actually changing the patterns of how we travel and holiday?

Throughout this book we are looking at things we can do in our own lives to see God's justice come in our world today.

We could be forgiven for thinking that perhaps we could take a break from this when it comes to having a holiday! It can be easy to view the money we pay for our holidays as partly paying for insulation from the poverty or environmental damage afflicting the countries we visit, and for the right to ignore the problems of indigenous people: paying for the right to take photos of poverty, but not to do anything about it. It is clear that we cannot have that luxury. In 'J is for Jobs' and 'S is for Simplicity' we saw that being involved in God's heart for justice is a holistic thing that encompasses every area of our lives.

There is nothing wrong with holidays. They can be much-needed times of rest and relaxation; times by ourselves or with family and friends; opportunities to see more of our amazing world and the people who live in it. Recent research from ABTA shows that people are becoming more aware of the ethical issues surrounding their holidays and more interested in ensuring that their holidays are responsible.[17] Let's make sure we are one of those people.

Action points

- Next time you book a holiday, make sure you enquire into it fully. For more details on questions to ask your tourist operator, and on campaigning on this issue more generally, contact Tearfund and Tourism Concern.

- Consider your flying habits and, if you fly regularly, look at how you might cut that down. If your work requires it, try talking to your boss about other modes of transport or methods of communication. Could being 'carbon neutral' become a company policy?

- Does your lifestyle demand regular holidays throughout the year? Think how you might build smaller 'pitstops' into your life to make you less holiday-reliant. Take one of those times when you might go away and stay at home instead, giving the money you would have spent to friends who cannot afford to go away so often.

Good contacts
Climate Care: 58 Church Way, Oxford OX4 4EF; 01865 777 770; <www.co2.org>
Tourism Concern: Stapleton House, 277–281 Holloway Road, London N7 8HN; 0207753 3330; <www.tourismconcern.org.uk>

A good book
M. Mann, *The Good Alternative Travel Guide*

U is for Unwanted Peoples

In this chapter we are going to meet four people: Kalim, Tamba, Amoru and Mandelena. Each one of them illustrates something of the situations faced by the world's most unwanted peoples: refugees.

Kalim came from a country ruled by a dictatorship. Ethnic conflicts and jealousies, provoked by the economic successes of the minority grouping, had led the majority group to use their political strength to gain dominance. Now the minority grouping was facing persecution and oppression. All the men were forced to do hard labour and family members were routinely murdered. One day Kalim saw one of his people being publicly beaten. Enraged by the injustice, he killed the perpetrator. When the dictator learned of this, he tried to kill Kalim. Kalim knew his only option was to flee, and he became a refugee in a nearby country.

Kalim is just one person among many facing similar difficulties. The refugee problem today is vast. Refugees are officially persons who are 'outside their country and cannot return owing to a well-founded fear of persecution because of their race, religion, nationality, political opinion or membership of a particular social group'.[1] The latest figures from the Office of the United Nations High Commissioner for Refugees (UNHCR) estimates there to be 12 million refugees. Of these, Afghanistan is by far the largest country of origin, accounting for some 3.8 million refugees (a third of the refugee population).[2] Asia hosts the largest overall population of refugees (5.8 million) while Africa hosts 3.3 million.[3]

War and ethnic conflicts are two of the main factors that cause people to become refugees. The war in Kosovo brought this home forcibly to those of us living in the UK. Suddenly, refugees weren't people on the other side of the world. They looked like us, wore the same clothes as us and needed to be brought into our own country for help. The civil war that raged in Burundi, and culminated in the Rwandan genocide in 1994, caused over 500,000 refugees to camp along Tanzania's western border in the most awful conditions, lacking food, water, sanitation and proper shelter, and facing the rampant spread of diseases such as cholera. In Afghanistan in the mid-1990s, under the Mujahidin, there were 4.5 million Afghan refugees. Now there are still 3.5 million, mostly in Pakistan and Iran.

Tamba and his family were facing starvation. Throughout the region, the crops had failed and there was no food. In desperation, Tamba sent his sons to the neighbouring country, where, he had heard, there was plenty of food. Through an amazing series of events, his sons met one of the members of the Government, who personally gave them permission to bring the whole family into the country and granted them a special permit to stay there until the famine was over.

Families make up a large proportion of the refugee population. Indeed, around 45% of refugees are under the age of seventeen.[4] Child refugees are extremely vulnerable. Tamba's sons, however, were exceptionally lucky. Liberia, for example, saw 60,000 people displaced in 2002 through cross-border conflict. Among these people are large numbers of children, who are at risk of family separation and are threatened by malnutrition and disease due to lack of access to food, water, sanitation and health services. Lack of income-earning opportunities forces many children into exploitative livelihoods such as joining fighting forces or prostitution, leaving them exposed to physical and sexual abuse.[5]

Tamba and his family were forced to seek refuge elsewhere because of wide-scale crop failure. Incredibly, more people become refugees through environmental disasters than for any other reason; it is thought that there are at least 25 million environmental refugees today. Most of these are in Sub-Saharan Africa, the Indian subcontinent, China, Mexico and Central America, and it is estimated that numbers could double by 2010.[6]

As a high-ranking army officer and the best friend of the son of the king, Amoru was able to enjoy all the luxuries of life. His situation fell apart, however, when his public popularity made him an enemy of the jealous king, who made three attempts at his life. Living in a country that gave him no access to the law, Amoru fled from the capital and became a fugitive in the surrounding hills.

Internally Displaced Persons (IDPs) leave their homes for

the same reasons as refugees, but stay within their own country. There are currently an estimated 20–25 million IDPs and they are a subject of huge concern for the international community.[7] Because they are still under the laws of the state from which they are fleeing they are especially vulnerable, 'falling between the cracks' of current humanitarian law and assistance.[8] In a country in the throes of civil war, much of the basic services may have been destroyed; there may be no well-organized camps to receive IDPs, and fighting may make it difficult for aid organizations to provide relief.[9] Thirteen million IDPs are children who have been forced to leave their homes because of armed conflict or violence. As a Save the Children report stated, 'Once displaced, many children spend at least six years away from their homes. Many live in fear, and are forced to move over and over again.'[10]

Mandelena became a refugee ten years ago with her family. During those ten years she lost both her husband and two sons. Eventually she decided to return to the rural area in her homeland, accompanied only by her daughter-in-law, who insisted on coming with her, although she was from an ethnic grouping different from Mandelena's. On returning home, however, it was clear that the outlook was not good. Overwhelmed by poverty, Mandelena's daughter-in-law was forced to beg from the men in the fields. All alone, she laid herself open to sexual abuse.

Voluntarily returning home is generally seen as the best solution for displaced people, and the majority of refugees do indeed prefer to return home if able to do so safely. In 2001, 786,000 refugees went home. Conditions can be very hard, however, if basic infrastructures are still inadequate or ethnic tensions still simmer underneath.

Mandelena's story has a positive ending: she and her mother-in-law were able to return home and a relative still living in the area looked after them. The plight of the majority of women refugees, though, is not so good. Forty-eight per cent of refugees are female and they make up over half of the population in refugee camps. (40% of all people of concern to the UNHCR – including IDPs – live in camps.)[11] Here they often face worse hardships than the men, rarely having a say in how a camp is run or where services such as water tanks or toilets are sited. While under the care of the UNHCR, three times as many boys as girls receive education.[12]

All the people in our stories were able to find refuge or return home. As travel and communication improve, however, so the number of those seeking remote asylum is increasing. In response, countries are becoming increasingly unwilling to accept refugees. When an emergency situation leads to a massive influx of refugees, local people and communities can find their resources and environment stripped. This happened in the Karagwe district of Tanzania during the Rwandan crisis, when the local people's farms were taken over by huts for the refugees and their trees were destroyed for firewood.[13] It is the poorer countries who bear the brunt of the global refugee problem, and the richer countries should recognize their responsibility to help.

Although the scale of the problem is peculiar to our time, refugees were known in the Bible. In fact, our four stories are all taken from biblical characters: Moses, Jacob and his sons, David, and Naomi and Ruth. We have already seen how the laws of the nation of Israel make particular reference to caring for those who are vulnerable, and this includes people from other countries – 'aliens'.[14] Moses' story is especially instructive because it is through the events that he led that the foundation for Israel's laws of compassion was laid. As Deuteronomy 10:18–19 shows, Israel is to love those who are aliens *because* they once were aliens too, in Egypt. Because of God's great compassion for them, so they are to show compassion to others (see also Is. 58:7 and Ezek. 22:7).

A wonderful demonstration of this is seen in the early church. The Christian apologist Aristides gives this description:

> They walk in all humility and kindness, and falsehood is not found among them, and they love one another. They don't despise the widow and don't upset the orphan. He who has gives liberally to him who has not. If they see a stranger, they bring him under their roof and rejoice over him, as it were their own brother: for they call themselves brethren, not after the flesh, but after the spirit and in God … And if there is among them a person who is poor and needy, and they have not an abundance of necessaries, they fast two or three days that they may supply the needy with their necessary food.

What an encouragement for us to live similarly!

Action point

- Sign up to receive the newsletters of some of the organizations involved in refugee issues: UNHCR or other overseas-development organizations that work with refugee communities abroad (e.g. Oxfam, Christian Aid, CAFOD, Save the Children, Church Mission Society, Médicins Sans Frontières). Allow your increased awareness to lead to other actions such as letter-writing or financial support.

Good contacts

Refugee Council: 3 Bondway, London SW8 1SJ; 020 7820 3145; <www.refugeecouncil.org.uk>. They also house *Student Action for Refugees (STAR)*.
UNHCR (UK): 21st Floor, Millbank Tower, 21–24 Millbank, London SW1P 4QP; 020 7932 019; <www.ukforunhcr.org>
Refugees Studies Centre: Queen Elizabeth House, University of Oxford, 21 St Giles, Oxford OX1 3LA; 01865 270722; <www.qeh.ox.ac.uk/rsc>

V is for Volunteers

My next-door neighbour is a vibrant teenage girl who, having coped with minor disabilities herself, wants to help children who are more severely disabled. While studying childcare at college, she gives one Saturday a month to helping at a playgroup for disabled children and, once a year, takes a whole week to help with a play-scheme. Lizzie isn't the only person I can think of who gives time for free. My mum volunteers as a bereavement councillor; one friend does hospital visiting, while another runs a local football team. One neighbour is a Neighbourhood Watch coordinator, and I'm Co-chair of our local estate Community Association. In fact, nearly half the adult population volunteers, putting in an average of four hours a week, contributing around £40 billion a year to the national economy.[1]

In 'J is for Jobs' we looked at the idea that our work covers a wide spectrum of activities, reaching beyond just what we are paid to do. This links in with our consideration of time in 'S is for Simplicity'. We are often encouraged to be generous with our money and it is a great privilege to be able to be generous also with our time, that oh-so-precious commodity.

Throughout the course of this book we have looked at a great many actions that we can take to be reaching for God's justice in our world. Giving our time is a fantastic way of making a difference to the people around us and to the planet on which we live. We could help in a children's club or at a homeless shelter; run a Traidcraft stall at church; work in a charity shop or help at a lunch club for elderly people. We could use our business skills to help a local charity. We could teach IT; decorate or garden for an old or disabled person; help to run an Alpha group; get involved in local environmental work; help to run an arts centre; build, cook, clean ... The opportunities are endless.

Volunteering is a great way of putting our natural or learnt skills to other uses. It gives us the scope to take the activities that we enjoy and use them for the benefit of others. It is a chance to do something completely different from our paid work.

There are also residential volunteering opportunities. This enables you to try things for a week or two or to dedicate a longer period of time to working with an organization, living away from home. You can spend time with a care organization, an environmental conservation group or a charity dedicated to animal welfare. There are also various Christian opportunities, such as L'Arche homes for people with disabilities, and the Lee Abbey retreat centre.[2]

For something completely different and very rewarding, try volunteering overseas. The traditional time to do this is during a gap year, between school and university or university and paid work.[3] I went to Malaysia for five months after my A-levels and worked with a Christian care association. The huge range of possibilities, however, means that this needn't be restricted to gap years. Overseas volunteering can be anything from one week to two years, but they will generally involve a cost, and many organizations will expect you to raise your own funds for the trip. Again, there are many Christian opportunities as well as secular ones.[4]

Anybody, anywhere, can be a volunteer. Whether you are young, a student, at home with small kids, disabled, retired or hard at work, there is something you can do to volunteer. Employer-supported volunteering is a good way to help those who are working to find the time to volunteer. The Body Shop, for example, encourages all its staff who work in the head office to take a regular half day to volunteer in the local community. If you're an employer, running a volunteering scheme can be very beneficial. It can lead to improved staff skills and confidence, with higher staff morale; to better team-building and a good public image.[5]

The benefits of volunteering are felt not only by employers who encourage their staff in that direction. Volunteering brings many benefits: the sheer enjoyment of the activity; the satisfaction of seeing results; meeting people; a sense of personal achievement; the chance to learn new skills or gain a qualification, and the opportunity to achieve a position in the community.[6] From a purely selfish motive it also looks great on your CV! Research by Reed Executive found that 70% of top businesses preferred to recruit candidates with volunteering on their CV.[7]

If the statistics are anything to go by, many readers of this book will be volunteers already. If you're not, consider whether you might have some time, however small, to give away. This chapter is perhaps the most practical outworking of all that we have been looking at so far and gives a genuine opportunity to make a real difference to a situation you feel passionate about.

Action points
- Use these questions to help yourself think through what you might like to do:
  1 How much time do you have a week for taking up a new commitment? Is that time in the evenings, at weekends or in the daytime?
  2 What do you like doing?
  3 What skills do you have?
  4 How much responsibility do you want to take on?

5 Are you more focused on local or on national issues?

6 List three local and three national issues that you are interested in. Do you already belong to, or have links with, groups that are taking up these issues?

7 Is there any particular group of people you are interested in?

8 What things do you not like doing?

9 Would you be prepared to put some money aside, either to help a cause or to provide yourself with information? If so, how much?

10 What do other people think about your plans? How will they fit in with family life? [8]

- Contact your local volunteer bureau to discuss with them what opportunities there are.

- Get hold of *TimeGuide* from <www.timebank.org.uk>.

Good contacts
The Besom: 2 Crosland Place, Taybridge Road, London SW11 5PJ; 020 7223 6544; <www.besom.com>
National Centre for Volunteering: Regent's Wharf, 8 All Saints St, London N1 9RL; 020 7520 8900; <www.volunteering.org.uk>
Volunteer Development England (formerly National Association of Volunteer Bureaux): New Oxford House, 16 Waterloo St, Birmingham B2 5UG; 0121 633 4555; <www.vde.org.uk>

W is for Water

With UK floods filling our newspapers at one time of the year and hosepipe bans coming into effect at other times, we get a small taster of the powerful issue that is water. Yet we think nothing of flushing the toilet, washing our hands, having a shower, filling the kettle ... Water is, literally, on tap. For those of us living in the economically developed countries, it is hard to imagine what it must be like not to have easy access to as much clean water as we like, and almost impossible to grasp that that is the reality for so many people today.

Currently 41% of the world's population (2.3 billion people) live in areas where there is 'water stress'. Out of these 2.3 billion people, 1.7 billion live in high water-stress areas where the consequences of water shortages are more acute, leading to problems with local food production and economic development.[1]

The situation looks set to worsen and it is thought that by 2025 two out of every three people will live in water-stressed areas.[2] Much of this is due to global demands, which are increasing at more than double the rate of population growth. The biggest share of the world's water goes to agriculture, which consumes 75%, while industry consumes 20% and the remaining 5% is used for domestic purposes.[3] Unfortunately, agricultural irrigation systems are often inefficient and waste huge amounts of water. Sometimes around 60% of irrigation water is lost to evaporation and runoff, never reaching the crops.[4]

As with so many environmental issues, it is the poor who suffer most but are least responsible for the problems. As competition for water increases, the rich and powerful are the ones who will win. One major cause of water shortages is the migration of people to the cities, leading to a demand that far outstrips supply as people desperately try to survive in slums and shanty towns. As the economic demands placed on poorer countries by the rich nations include the privatization of public amenities, so water prices are hiked up in the cities and the needs of those in urban areas are ignored.[5] Water problems are becoming more severe, too, because of the increasing consumption of water due to economic development and growing standards of living. As we have seen already, the tourism industry can make shortages worse as hotels and golf-courses take most of the water away from the local community.[6] The health implications are catastrophic, while armed conflict over dwindling water resources, particularly in the Middle East, will become an increasing threat.

In the UK we are fortunate not to suffer extreme water shortages to the extent that other countries do.[7] Water is not, however, the limitless resource that we often think it is. The average person in the UK uses 1,050 litres of water a week and the result is that the natural water-tables are lowering.[8] Not taking into consideration the potential problems that climate change will cause, the National Rivers Authority predicts that by 2021 there will be a deficit in water supply in the Severn Trent, Thames and Anglian regions and, should water demand increase more severely, the Wessex region will also be in deficit. The World Resources Institute has graded countries according to water availability per capita, and, interestingly, the UK is deemed 'low', in the same category as South Africa.[9]

As well as having a devastating impact on the lives of people around the world, the shortage of freshwater is also severely affecting the ecosystems that rely on it. In the UK, for example, over-extraction is threatening rivers in many regions, leaving water levels too low to sustain their wildlife populations. An English Nature survey found one in ten freshwater wetland Sites of Special Scientific Interest (SSSIs) in England to be threatened by water extraction, and Friends of the Earth have identified over 250 SSSIs in England and Wales that are being similarly affected.[10] Repeated the world over, this is leading to a very worrying decline in the wildlife that these places support. The Freshwater Species Population Index, which measures the average change over time in the populations of 194 species of freshwater birds, mammals, reptiles, amphibians and fish, fell by nearly 50% between 1970 and 1999.

139

Around the world, it is the building of dams to provide water that is causing the most damage. There are currently 45,000 large dams on the world's rivers.[11] A dam causes huge problems to the hydrological cycle of a river and hence to its ecosystem. The World Commission on Dams found that over 60% of the large dams it surveyed had significant problems with disrupted fish migrations.[12] Alongside dams are the problems associated with providing water for irrigation. Perhaps the best-known example is the Aral Sea in the former Soviet Union, which has shrunk to less than half its original size due to the diversion of two inflowing rivers in order to provide irrigation water for local croplands.[13]

Alongside the issue of water shortage is the extremely pressing problem of pollution and water sanitation. Twenty per cent of the world's population doesn't have access to safe drinking water. The result is that water-borne diseases from faecal pollution is a major cause of illness in developing countries. Polluted water is thought to affect the health of 1.2 billion people, and contributes to the death of 15 million children annually.[14]

Faecal pollution remains a large cause of poor water

quality in developing countries, and this, combined with new pollutants such as pesticides, are heavily degrading water, particularly around urban industrial centres and intensive agricultural areas. It is estimated that 90% of waste water in developing countries is discharged directly into rivers and streams without any waste-processing treatment.[15]

In more industrialized countries a new range of pollutants keeps rivers and underground water supplies contaminated. One of the biggest causes of pollution is intensive agriculture. The large amount of chemicals used means that some of it leaks into groundwater and rivers. Poisonous to wildlife, these chemicals can build up in plants and animals, with the result that those animals at the top of their food chains, such as herons and otters, accumulate high levels of pesticides in their bodies. The increased use of manure and manufactured fertiliser leads to dangerous levels of nitrates and phosphorous. As we saw in 'K is for Kippers', these act as fertilisers themselves and promote algal blooms (the process of eutrophication), which deoxygenates the water, killing fish through suffocation.[16] Industry, lead piping, sewage and the liquid that leaks out from landfill sites all contribute to a global situation of degraded water quality.

As with so many of the issues we have looked at in this book, the problems here are huge and often beyond our control. Yet there are always things we can do to ensure that we are playing our part positively.

On a global level, we come back to 'L is for Letters' and our role in supporting the work of organizations by campaigning. This may mean writing to the big water companies, asking them to act responsibly when water is privatized in poorer nations. It might mean writing to our own Government, urging them to meet the targets on sanitation agreed at the Johannesburg Summit on Sustainable Development.[17]

At a local level there are steps we can all take to reduce the amount of water we use. We use the most water in flushing our toilets (31%), so finding ways to reduce our usage here will have a large effect. When I was in America recently, staying in an area where water was precious, the toilets had a sign over them that read, 'If it's yellow let it mellow, if it's brown flush it down.' Putting a brick or a 'Hippo bag' in your cistern and buying a dual-flush toilet when replacing an old one will also be effective.

After toilets, the greatest amount of water is used in personal washing (26%), then by washing machines (12%) and then in washing up (10%).[18] With this in mind, we should make sure we shower instead of have a bath, turn the tap off while brushing our teeth and use our washing machines or dishwashers only when full (or wash up by hand). Water butts, of course, are a great way of saving rainwater for use on the garden; we can also use 'grey' water, in which we've washed ourselves, our dishes or our vegetables.

Access to clean water is the most basic need we have. No wonder the final picture in Revelation is of 'the river of the water of life, as clear as crystal, flowing from the throne of God and of the Lamb' (Rev. 22:1)! All of us need to do what we can to ensure that every person in our world has access, not only to the heavenly water, but also to the earthly 'water of life'.

Action points

- Write one letter that will support the work of one of the organizations below regarding water.

- Make a note every time you use water today. Think through what you could do to use less.

- Look back at 'O is for Organic' and 'F is for Food'. Since so much water pollution is from chemicals, here is another reason to become as 'organic' as possible.

Good contacts
Friends of the Earth: see 'C is for Creation'
Tearfund: see 'A is for Activists'
WaterAid: Prince Consort House, 27–29 Albert
Embankment, London SE1 7UB; 020 7793 4500;
<www.wateraid.org.uk>
The Waterways Trust: North West Office, The Boat Museum,
South Pier Road, Ellesmere Port CH65 4FW; 0845 0700 710;
<www.thewaterwaystrust.co.uk>

X is for Xenophobia

The convenience store on my estate used to be run by an
Iranian man. After years of harassment he has eventually
managed to sell the shop and move on. It was all small-scale
stuff: graffiti on the walls, damage done to signs, verbal
abuse. The worst thing was an envelope of cockroaches put
through the letterbox once. Over years, though, it all adds up.
Now the shop is run by a Nigerian couple, who are beginning
to experience the same things. It can be no coincidence that,
of the four shops on the estate, the two run by white people
have no problems, whereas Moses' shop and the Indian
takeaway suffer constantly.

By contrast, Phoenix Community Care, based at a church
in north London and working with Haringey Council, offer
accommodation for unaccompanied asylum-seekers under the

age of sixteen. The young people are placed together in houses that PCC has bought, and each one is assigned a key worker, who spends time with them, helping with application forms, legal situations and the general problems of being in a strange country. The stories coming from these young people, both of the situations they have left and of the treatment they received on entering the UK, are often horrendous. But this local church treats each one with the dignity and care that they deserve.[1]

Xenophobia – or racism – happens all around the globe and is the cause of most of the terrible atrocities that we witnessed last century, whether in Russia, Vietnam, Germany, Rwanda or Kosovo. While, in the UK, racism is not primarily a 'black versus white' issue, on a global level we have the situation where, as David Haslam says, with its colonial roots 'the poverty line is the colour line, everywhere. Black [or brown, or yellow] almost always means poor ... white means wealthy'.[2] This fact has been evident throughout the book; so many of the issues that we have been considering, such as HIV or water, predominantly affect people who are not white. Many of us reading this who are white may feel pretty confident that we aren't racist. But one of the challenges of this book is to consider where we may yet be contributing to global racism and how we can begin to change that.

The main focus of this chapter, though, is on racism in the UK. However much the situation may have improved, life on my estate shows me that racism is still alive and well.[3] The UK is becoming increasingly multi-ethnic. In 2001/2 the size of the minority ethnic population was 4.5 million: 7.6% of the total population of the UK. People of Indian descent are the largest group, followed by individuals of Pakistani, Black Caribbean and Black African descent and those of multi-ethnic backgrounds. In England people from minority ethnic groups make up 9% of the population (compared with only 2% in Scotland and Wales). Nearly half (48%) live in London, where they comprise 29% of all residents.[4] In Haringey, the most culturally diverse borough, the council reckons that over 190 languages are spoken.

One important issue for minority ethnic groups in Britain is employment and income. People in minority ethnic groups have higher unemployment rates than people of British descent, and Bangladeshi people have the highest (20% and 24% for men and women respectively). Just over 40% of Bangladeshi men aged under 25 are unemployed, compared with 12% of young men of British descent. Not surprisingly, therefore, Pakistani and Bangladeshi households are more reliant on social security benefits, which make up 19% of their gross income. Overall, people from minority ethnic groups are more likely than people of British descent to live in low-income households. Indeed, almost 60% of Pakistani and Bangladeshi people live in low-income households.[5]

We have a Chinese student from Hong Kong living with us. Last year, as he was walking along the road, he was attacked by a group of white teenagers, for no other reason than for being a 'Chinky'. His injuries put him in hospital. While only 0.3% of white people risk being the victims of a racially motivated incident, 4.2% of Pakistani and Bangladeshi people, 3.6% of Indian people and 2.2% of black people find themselves at risk.[6] Alongside unemployment and income issues, racially motivated crime and the attitude of the police and judicial system are equally concerning.

My experiences have all been positive. Alan, our Chinese friend, recently testified in court against his attackers and saw them prosecuted. The family at the centre of the racism directed against the Iranian shop-owner were evicted by the housing association and the main protagonist was sent to prison. Similarly, two men on the estate who were violent towards workers at the Indian takeaway have also ended up in prison as a result.

For many, however, the experience is not so positive. Mal and Linda Hussain, who run a small business on an estate in Lancaster, have faced graffiti, bricks through the windows, fire-bombings, death threats, violent assaults and constant verbal abuse. The authorities have been very slow to react. Mal and Linda began to keep a detailed record of the harassment, recording each incident and logging their calls to the police. Eventually some of the perpetrators began to be successfully prosecuted, although mainly for relatively minor offences. There have now been nearly forty successful prosecutions, but the abuse still continues and none of the perpetrators have yet been evicted from their council homes on the estate.[7]

While many problems still persist, overall the situation seems to be improving. A key to this is the media. In February 2002, an encouraging report was published that found that attitudes towards, and the presentation and inclusion of, people from minority ethnic groups have considerably bettered over recent years.[8] The report found, however, that negative attitudes have now shifted on to asylum-seekers. The British media now exhibit some of the most hostile attitudes compared to our European counterparts, and the report criticized the British media for their xenophobic and intolerant coverage of asylum issues.[9]

Those of us reading this will represent many different views regarding Britain's asylum policies. Countries and nationalities are important in giving people a sense of security and identity. If immigration controls are too open and the labour market becomes flooded, the finite resources of the welfare and education system will break down, unable to cope with the numbers. Nevertheless, we must acknowledge that 'all immigration controls are ... based to some degree on xenophobia and racism – we want to retain our patch of Earth for people like us'.[10] We must bear this in mind when we consider that those countries to whom we owe a particular historical allegiance (in the Caribbean, the Indian subcontinent and East and West Africa), whose citizens may often have families and friends in the UK, are facing increasingly restricted access to Britain, whereas our (white) European neighbours are able to come, go and work in the UK as they like.

The fact is that the UK does not receive as many asylum-seekers as some parts of the media claim.[11] In 2001 there were 71,365 applications, compared with over 900,000 asylum-seekers worldwide. Out of fifteen EU countries, Britain ranks eighth in terms of asylum applicants per 1,000 inhabitants. The UK asylum system is far from being a 'soft touch' and has inherent problems, leading to many asylum-seekers' being refused application with no enquiry into whether they might be facing persecution or death when returned home.[12] More positively, refugees and asylum-seekers have much to contribute to the UK, both financially and culturally. A recent Home Office report estimated that, in 1999/2000, migrants in the UK contributed £2.5 billion, equivalent to saving 1p on the basic rate of income tax.[13] The reality is that, because of population decline, we need immigrants, not least to bring in their professional expertise – for example, into our hospitals.

Despite this, racism demonstrated towards asylum-seekers and refugees can make their lives a misery. Many asylum-seekers arrive in a state of shock or trauma from horrific experiences, yet do not find support on entering the UK. A report by Refugee Action on women's experiences of asylum showed that newly arrived refugee women feel so unsafe in the UK that 83% live under self-imposed curfew, locking themselves indoors by 7pm. Eighty-four per cent live in accommodation with no telephone and 30% have been verbally or physically abused, including being spat on or shouted at. Seventy per cent of refugee women are without a husband, having been separated or widowed by conflict, and 37% of those who are mothers are separated from their children.[14]

In 'A is for Activists' and elsewhere, we have noted the foundational principle that all people have been made in the image of God. One nation, Israel, was explicitly chosen to be 'his people' in order that all nations might be redeemed (Is. 49:6). God is manifestly the God and creator of all people, and the Old Testament is not frightened to show God moving beyond the boundaries of his chosen people (for example, in the stories of Ruth and Jonah and in the description of Cyrus, king of Persia, as his 'anointed' [Is. 45:1]).

In 'G is for Globalization' we saw the global vision that the Bible has, culminating in the great multitude worshipping before the throne, from every nation, tribe, people and language (Rev. 7:9). The Day of Pentecost (Acts 2) is a wonderful outworking of this picture, as are Peter's vision and the subsequent conversion of the Gentile Cornelius in Acts 10:9–48. In both we see that God's power and salvation are for all; there is no favouritism (see also Gal. 3:26–28; Col. 3:11).

Our supreme model is Jesus, who refused to let racial boundaries stand in the way of God's love (see e.g. Matt. 8:5–13; Matt. 15:21–28; Luke 9:51–55 and the parable of the good Samaritan in Luke 10). Writing on 'loving the stranger', the Revd Dr Inderjit Bhogal says, 'Jesus has left an example for his community. Practise hospitality. Eat with each other. Eat with the most vulnerable ones. Eat with "the stranger". Our lifestyle should be one of hospitality and solidarity, not hostility and segregation.'[15] As Abraham showed hospitality to the three strangers in Genesis 18, so we too should be ready to open our doors to those who are not like ourselves. The Chief Rabbi, Dr Jonathan Sacks, quotes the Jewish sages who said, 'On only one occasion does the Hebrew Bible command us to love our neighbour, but in 37 places commands us to love the stranger', and, he adds, 'The stranger is one we are taught to love precisely because he is not like ourselves.'[16] This is hard, and often we fear getting to know people who are different. Yet we need to be willing to try and, regarding asylum-seekers, we must be open-minded as to who is genuine and who is not.

As people following Jesus, racism cannot be something we tolerate. We must all take steps to see it eradicated.[17]

Action points

- Increase your awareness of ethnic minority issues. Keep a lookout for relevant television and radio programmes and sign up to receive a regular paper such as *The Voice, Caribbean Times* or *Asian Times*.

- If 'V is for Volunteering' whetted your appetite, you could consider volunteering for a local asylum-seekers' project or visiting an immigration detainee (see AVID's details below).

- Encourage your church to hold a Racial Justice Sunday each year (usually around September) and, from that, to get more involved in racism issues. For more details contact CCRJ (see below).

Good contacts

Association of Visitors to Immigration Detainees (AVID): PO Box 7, Oxted, Surrey RH8 0YT; 01883 712713; <ireland@hj44.freeserve.co.uk>
Churches Commission for Racial Justice (CCRJ): Inter-Church House, 35–41 Lower Marsh, London SE1 7SA; 020 7523 2121; <www.ctbi.org.uk/ccrj>
Refugee Council: see 'U is for Unwanted People'

Good books
R. Beckford, *Jesus is Dread*
D. Haslam, *Race for the Millennium*
B. C. Parekh, *The Future of Multi-Ethnic Britain*

Y is for Young people

One of the primary reasons for setting up the Community Association that I co-chair was to help the young people on our estate. Over a number of years, residents had noticed growing problems from a specific group of young people: drug and alcohol abuse, physical and verbal violence against residents, petty crime and general antisocial behaviour. The problems on the estate are nothing new and have all the classic symptoms, with a high rate of teenage pregnancy, broken families, low education and little prospects, and just plain boredom.

The Community Association is working hard to see things change. We've formed a Community Action Project with the police, local council, youth service and housing association to ensure that these agencies are seeing the estate as a priority and coordinating their efforts to combat antisocial behaviour. We have had a five-a-side and basketball area built on the green in the middle of the estate and a youth shelter built next to it to provide a place where they can hang out, away from the 'hot spots'. We have just received funding for two youth workers to work on the estate for a year, to listen to what the young people regard as their needs. One of the workers belongs to my church and is linked in with wider youth projects, and so has access to many different resources. As I write this, we are applying for funding to have a 'Football in the Community' scheme in the summer, run by players from Brighton and Hove Albion, which not only teaches football but also focuses on other lifestyle issues, such as health, discipline and respect for others. We don't expect to work miracles overnight, but, if we achieve nothing else, at least we shall show the young people that they are worth spending time and money on.

Of course, the issues on my estate are nothing new and are mirrored around the country. In fact, the problems on my estate are nothing compared with those faced by many others elsewhere. In 2000, of an under-fifteen UK population of 12 million, 4 million were classed as 'vulnerable': at risk of exclusion or living in poor circumstances. Four hundred thousand were classified as being 'in need', meaning in serious circumstances; 53,000 were Looked After and 32,000 were on the Child Protection Register.[1] Up to 70% of young people in foster care and over 80% in residential care leave school with no qualifications.[2] A Department of Health survey of 10,000 5-to-15-year-olds revealed that 10% had a mental health problem. Three in every 5 children in every classroom have witnessed domestic violence and, in 1999, 12% of 11-to-15-year-olds reported using drugs in the previous year. In an NSPCC survey of 3,000 18-to-24-year-olds, 7% reported abuse and 43% reported bullying.[3]

Perhaps the biggest issue facing our young people is the consumerism that we looked at in 'G is for Globalization' and 'N is for Needs'. Commercialization is getting hold of children from a very young age, leading to the pressures of branding and needing to be part of the MTV generation. Through the marketing of brands comes its sexualization, and there is a constant battle to maintain the innocence and purity of youth.

Whatever the problems, however, there are actions that all of us can take, and none of us lives in an area that is entirely isolated from these issues. Most simply, we can be friendly. How many of us reading this book would cite a youth worker, church leader, neighbour or teacher as having played a large part in our development as children and teenagers, both positively and negatively? One of the most striking aspects of juvenile crime figures is the small percentage of young people who commit the highest number of crimes. What a difference could be made if these young people were able to form relationships with people who would help them through life![4]

When I was little, my mum looked out of her front window one winter's day to see two young girls standing out in the snow. When they were still there some time later, Mum went out and talked to them, and discovered that their mum had shoved them outside first thing in the morning and told them not to come back till evening. Mum invited them inside, and that was the start of a friendship with them that lasted all the way through their teens. They still pop in from time to time to say hello. They have had a rough life, but I wonder what else might have happened to them had they not had my mum to be a steady influence as they grew up.

It is also good for adults to remember that young people are more than capable of being a positive force for good themselves and are very good at making a difference. Cred, for example, ran a conference on human rights in Westminster for schools in London. Two sixth-form students, in par-ticular, found the topics interesting and decided to volunteer to help at future events. This led to their chairing a confer-ence – attended by Gordon Brown, Hilary Benn (Minister for

International Development) and Jan Vandemoortele (of the UN Development Programme) – which looked at how to reach the UN's Millennium Goals of halving child poverty by 2015.

In the UK we are facing the problems of a population consisting of too few young people and too many old people. In many places around the world, however, the reverse is the case. In fact, the current generation of people under eighteen is the largest in the history of the world; more than a fifth of the world's population is aged between ten and nineteen. When one considers that about 85% of adolescents live in developing countries, and that 600 million children and adolescents grow up in families surviving on incomes of less than 70p ($1) a day, it becomes clear that the problems faced by young people are immense.[5]

In 'H is for HIV', we saw the shocking statistic that Aids will eventually kill half of all fifteen-year-old Ethiopian, South African and Zimbabwean boys. Indeed, every fifty seconds a child dies of an Aids-related illness and another becomes infected.[6] The Aids pandemic is hindering the advances in child survival, health and education that have been gained by many countries. Particularly in Sub-Saharan Africa, which is home to around two-thirds of people with HIV, the effects of the virus on young people are devastating.[7]

Aids is not the only health issue facing young people across the world. Of the 11 million children under five who die each year, most die from preventable diseases such as pneumonia, diarrhoea, malaria and measles.[8] Water sanitation issues, which we looked at in 'W is for Water', and malnutrition, caused by poverty, are majority factors in these deaths.[9] Measures that we take for granted – such as immunization, an emphasis on breastfeeding and the consumption of iodized salt (to combat iodine deficiency disorders that leads to mental impairment) – are crucial in seeing the health of our world's young people improve.[10]

Running parallel to issues of health is that of education. Although primary-school enrolment is increasing, still 100 million primary-school-aged children are out of school (60% of them girls).[11] In Somalia, as few as 21% of boys and 13% of girls attend primary school.[12] It hardly needs to be said how important good education is, both to the well-being of the individual – developing qualities and giving them skills that can help them avoid dangers such as bonded labour or armed recruitment – and to the development of a country, which can be transformed in a single generation where education is improved.

153

Crucial to both the health and education of young people is the status of women in a society. It is no coincidence that, looking at a map showing women's literacy rates, nearly all the countries with under 30% are in Africa.[13] Where women are valued girls are valued, and where girls are valued the education and health of all young people are improved.

Young people face many hazards today. Armed conflict places young people in extremely vulnerable positions.[14] Issues around young people working – whether in sweat-shops, bonded labour or in the sex industry – continue to cause untold damage to millions of lives.[15]

Whether it is these issues or others, such as street children, the underlying problem is the same: poverty. It is a sad fact that a young person's prospects for survival and development depend on where he or she was born. In particular, external debts have a direct impact as money is taken away from health and education and from fighting the other problems young people face. To see the lives of young people around the world set free from the tyranny of fear and deprivation, we must push for the cancellation of unsustainable debt (with strings attached to ensure the money reaches those most in need). We must press for developed countries to increase their aid budget to countries locked in poverty, and for macro-economic and fiscal policies to have young people as a key focus.

The good news is that, wherever there are young people in trouble, there are people working to see matters change. One woman I know has moved out to South Africa to work with babies abandoned on the streets of Johannesburg. Cred supports a primary school in the slums of Addis Ababa, Ethiopia, that has been specifically set up for street children. Between 1998 and 2003, money from our supporters has enabled 600 children to attend that school. Another of our partners, Women at Risk, also in Addis Ababa, works with young prostitutes, giving them vocational and life-skills training and helping them to move out of the sex trade. There is so much that needs to be done, but also so much that is being done to see situations change. We can all be a part of that.

Action points

- Think about the young people in your neighbourhood or church. Are their needs and potential being met? Is there anything you can do, even if it's just being a friendly face? Perhaps 'V is for Volunteering' has already inspired you to do something!

- If you do not already do so, consider supporting an organization that works with young people, whether at home or abroad. The list is endless, but we've met some organizations already in other chapters: e.g. Cred ('A is for Activists'), Phoenix Community Care ('X is for Xeno-phobia') and HopeHIV ('H is for HIV'). See also the Viva Network (details below).

Good contacts
Barnardos: Tanners Lane, Barkingside, Ilford, Essex
IG6 1QG; 020 8551 6870; <www.barnardos.org.uk>
Oasis: 115 Southwark Bridge Road, London SE1 0AX;
020 7450 9000; <www.oasistrust.org>
Save the Children: 17 Grove Lane, London SE5 8RD;
020 7703 5400; <www.savethechildren.org.uk>
UNICEF: 3 United Nations Plaza, H-9F, New York NY 10017,
USA; <www.unicef.org>
Viva Network: PO Box 633, Oxford OX2 0XZ; 01865
320100; <www.viva.org>
YMCA England: 640 Forest Rd, London, E17 3DZ; 020 8520
5599; <www.ymca.org.uk>

Z is for Zeitgeist

On a CD cover recently I read this:

> 'What is 'Zeitgeist?' we are continually quizzed. 'Spirit of the time',
> we nod, trying to look the part. 'Era defining', we occasionally add
> as a bit of a try on. We'll tell you what it is ... It's trying to make
> some sense of the glorious mess that is acid house.[1]

Throughout this book we have been 'trying to make some
sense', not of a particular genre of music, but of 'the glorious mess' that is our world. 'Glorious mess' wonderfully

encapsulates what we see as we consider the many different topics that make up this book.

There is no doubt that we live in a beautiful world. Just consider the amazing beauty of the rainforests or the coral reefs; the skylark spiralling over the fields or the water vole swimming through the rivers. As humans, too, we have been richly blessed with the ability to form friendships and nurture our families; with the means to travel and trade throughout the world, creating wealth and prosperity; with opportunities to develop our talents and potential, enhancing our sense of well-being.

This most certainly is glorious. As we see continually, these blessings come from God, who loves giving us good things. As we use them well, so the glory goes back to him.

But we also live in a mess. The spirit of the age blinds us to the origin of these good things, turns us away from our relationships and into ourselves, and causes us to see these gifts as being our own, to be used for our own ends. As with the good, so with the evil. It runs through every chapter of this book: greed and exploitation, selfishness and idolatry.

As people who don't want to conform to the spirit of the age, but want to be transformed by the renewing of our minds (Rom. 12:2), we must look critically at the blessings we have received and ensure that we are using them to bless others. The danger is that we can become hypnotized by our cultural norms and blinded to the possibilities we have to see change.[2]

The good news is that there *is* an alternative. The gospel has the power to break that hypnotism and enables us to change our lives so that they may reflect the goodness of God and his blessing for his creation. In essence, what we are talking about here is moving from the spirit of the age to the kingdom of God, pictures of which we have looked at a number of times.[3] As we do this we move from the values of this age and towards the values of the kingdom: values of selflessness and peace, of inclusivity and love.

The kingdom of God is made visible through our prayers; through the concentrations of our worship; through our practice of the disciplines and the cultivation of the Christian virtues. The kingdom is also made visible on this earth through our actions. Each time we can be bothered to send off a campaign postcard, each time we look up and smile at a neighbour, each time we buy a fair-trade product or take the trouble to leave the car at home we are playing our part in seeing God's kingdom come, now and into the future.[4]

This book has been a call to change our lives in order to respond to the many challenges facing our world. The changes facing us are many and varied: for some they are easily implemented while for others they demand wholesale adjustments. Whether we decide to write a letter every month, move our investments, buy more organic produce or revolutionize our working situation – whether these decisions we make take us a month to carry out or the rest of our lives – the gospel of Jesus fills us with hope and with the confidence that these changes are worth making. By doing so we are building into God's promised future, when there will be no more sickness or suffering, tears or death, and when all of God's creation will freely worship him.

Bibliography

Books

Atkinson, D., et al. (eds.) (1995), *New Dictionary of Christian Ethics and Pastoral Theology*, Leicester: IVP.

Barbour, B. (1995, 1996), *Jihad Versus McWorld: How Globalism and Tribalism are Reshaping the World*, New York: Ballantine Books.

Bauckham R., and Hart, T. (1999), *Hope Against Hope: Christian Eschatology in Contemporary Context*, London: Darton, Longman & Todd.

Beckford, R. (1998), *Jesus is Dread*, London: Darton, Longman and Todd.

Benton, J. (1999), *Christians in a Consumer Culture*, Fearn: Christian Focus Publications.

Berry, R. J. (ed.) (2000), *The Care of Creation*, Leicester: IVP.

—— (2003), *God's Book of Works*, London: T. & T. Clark.

Blomberg, C. (1999), *Neither Poverty Nor Riches: A Biblical Theology of Possessions*, Leicester: Apollos.

Blythman, J. (1999), *The Food Our Children Eat*, London: Fourth Estate.

Bruges, J. (2000), *The Little Earth Book*, Bristol: Alisdair Sawday Publishing.

Cootsona, G. (2002), *Creation and Last Things: At the Intersection of Theology and Science*, Louisville, KT: Geneva Press.

Department for International Development (2000), *Eliminating Poverty: Making Globalization Work for the Poor*, London: The Stationery Office.

Dominguez, J., and Robin, V. (1999), *Your Money or Your Life*, Harmondsworth: Penguin.

Dumbrell, W. J. (1984), *Covenant and Creation: A Theology of the Old Testament Covenants*, Grand Rapids, MI: Baker.

The Ecologist, Go M.A.D! 365 Daily Ways to Save the Planet, London: Think Publishing.

Fearnley-Whittingstall, H. (2001), *The River Cottage Cookbook*, London: HarperCollins.

Foster, R. (1995), *Freedom of Simplicity*, London: Triangle.

—— (1992), *Prayer: Finding the Heart's True Home*, London: Hodder & Stoughton.

Gnanakan, K. (1999), *God's World: A Theology of the Environment*, London: SPCK.

Goudzwaard, B. (2001), *Globalization and the Kingdom of God*, Washington, DC: Centre for Public Justice.

Greene, M. (2001), *Thank God it's Monday: Ministry in the Workplace*, London: Scripture Union.

Gunton, C. (1992), *Christ and Creation*, Carlisle: Paternoster.

Hamilton, G. (1991), *The Organic Garden Book*, London: Dorling Kindersley.

Haslam, D. (1996), *Race for the Millennium: A Challenge to Church and Society*, London: Church House.

Haugen, G. (1999), *Good News About Injustice*, Leicester: IVP.

Hengel, M. (1979), 'Property and Riches in the Early Church' in idem, *Earliest Christianity*, London: SCM.

Heslam, P. (2002), *Globalization: Unravelling the New Capitalism*, Cambridge: Grove.

Humphrys, J. (2001), *The Great Food Gamble*, London: Hodder & Stoughton.

Jones, J. (2003), *Jesus and the Earth*, London: SPCK.

Kraybill, D. (1978), *The Upside-down Kingdom*, Basingstoke: Marshalls.

Legrain, P. (2002), *Open World: The Truth About Globalization*, London: Abacus.

Luhrs, J. (1997), *The Simple Living Guide*, [PLACE]: Broadway Books.

McClaren, D., Bullock, S., and Yousuf, N. (1998), *Tomorrow's World: Britain's Share in a Sustainable Future*, London: Earthscan.

McCloughry, R. (1990), *Taking Action: The Practical Guide to Making an Impact in Society*, Leicester: Frameworks.

—— (1995), 'Community Ethics', in Atkinson et al. (eds.) (1995).

McFague, S. (1997), *Super, Natural Christians: How We Should Love Nature*, Minneapolis, MN: Augsburg Fortress.

Mann, M. (2002), *The Good Alternative Travel Guide: Exciting Holidays for Responsible Travellers*, Oxford: Oxford Educational.

Marine Conservation Society (2002), *Good Fish Guide: The Ultimate Consumer Guide to Eating 'Eco-friendly' Fish*.

Marshall, P. A. (1995), 'Work', in Atkinson et al. (eds.) (1995).

Micklethwait, J., and Wooldridge, A. (2000), *A Future Perfect: The Challenge and Hidden Promise of Globalisation*, London: Heinemann.

Moltmann, J. (2002), *Theology of Hope*, London: SCM.

Motyer, J. A. (1993), *The Prophecy of Isaiah*, Leicester: IVP.

Northcott, M. (1996), *The Environment and Christian Ethics*, Cambridge: Cambridge University Press.

—— (1999), *Life After Debt: Christianity and Global Justice*, London: SPCK.

Odgers, J., and Valerio, R. (2004), *Simplicity, Love and Justice*, London: Alpha International.

Osborn, L. (1993), *Guardians of Creation: Nature in Theology and the Christian Life*, Leicester: Apollos.

Pareck, P. C., and the Runnymede Trust Commission on the Future of Multi-Ethnic Britain (2000), *The Future of Multi-Ethnic Britain: The Report of the Commission on the Future of Multi-Ethnic Britain*, London: Profile.

Prance, G. (1996), *The Earth Under Threat*, Glasgow: Wild Goose.

Reed, C. (ed.) (2001), *Development Matters: Christian Perspectives on Globalization*, London: Church House.

Roddick, A. (ed.) (2001), *Take it Personally: How Globalization Affects You and Powerful Ways to Challenge It*, London: HarperCollins.

Rosner, B. (1999), *How to Get Really Rich: A Sharp Look at the Religion of Greed*, Leicester: IVP.

Sacks, J. (1995), *Faith in the Future*, London: Darton, Longman & Todd.

Samuel, V., and Sugden, C. (eds.) (1999), *Mission as Transformation: A Theology of the Whole Gospel*, Oxford: Regnum.

Schut, M. (ed.) (1999), *Simpler Living, Compassionate Life*, Denver: Living the Good News.

Semlyen, A. (2000), *Cutting Your Car Use: Save Money, Be Healthy, Be Green!*, Totnes: Green Books.

Sider, R. (1997), *Rich Christians in an Age of Hunger*, London: Hodder & Stoughton.

Sine, T. (1999), *Mustard Seed versus McWorld: Reinventing Life and Faith for the Future*, London: Monarch.

Sine, T., and Sine, C. (2002), *Living on Purpose: Finding God's Best for Your Life*, London: Monarch.

Starkey, M. (1989), *Born to Shop*, London: Monarch.

Stiglitz, J. (2002), *Globalization and Its Discontents*, London: Penguin.

Storkey, E. (1995), *The Search for Intimacy*, London: Hodder & Stoughton.

Stott, J. (1990), *Issues Facing Christians Today: New Perspectives on Social and Moral Dilemmas*, London: Marshall Pickering.

—— (1996), *Making Christ Known: Historic Mission Documents from the Lausanne Movement 1974–1989*, Carlisle: Paternoster.

Sugden, C. (2000), *Gospel, Culture and Transformation*, Oxford: Regnum.

Tanqueray, R. (2000), *Eco Chic: Organic Living*, London: Carlton.

Tiplady, R. (ed.) (2003), *One World or Many? Globalization and World Mission*, Pasadena, CA: William Carey Library.

Tondeur, K. (1998) *What Jesus Said About Money and Possessions*, London: Monarch.

Taylor, W. (ed.) (2000), *Global Missiology for the Twenty-first Century: from the Iguassu Dialogue*, Grand Rapids, MI: Baker.

UNHCR (2001), *Statistical Yearbook 2001*, Geneva: UNHCR.

—— (2002), *Statistical Yearbook 2002*, Geneva: UNHCR.

UNICEF (2000), *The State of the World's Children 2000*, New York: UNICEF.

—— (2001), *The State of the World's Children 2001*, New York: UNICEF.

—— (2002), *The State of the World's Children 2002*, New York: UNICEF.

Van Straten, M. (2001), *Organic Living*, London: Francis Lincoln.

Von Ruhland, C. (1997), *Louder than Words: An A-Z of Christian Social Action*, London: Triangle.

Warren, R. (2002) *The Purpose-driven Life: What on Earth Am I Here For?*, Grand Rapids, MI: Zondervan.

Wilkinson, D. (2002), *The Message of Creation*, Leicester: IVP.

Wolfe, J. (ed.) (1995), *Evangelical Faith and Public Zeal: Evangelicals and Society in Britain 1780–1980*, London: SPCK.

Wright, C. J. H. (1983) *Living as the People of God: The Relevance of Old Testament Ethics*, Leicester: IVP.

Wright, N. T. (1997), *For All God's Worth*, London: Triangle.

—— (1999), *New Heavens, New Earth: The Biblical Picture of Christian Hope*, Cambridge: Grove.

Other material

ABTA and Tearfund (2002), 'Improving Tour Operator Performance: The Role of Corporate Social Responsibility and Reporting'.

Black, R. (2001), 'Environmental Refugees: Myth or Reality?', Working Paper no. 34 for UNHCR. Supplied by the Refugee Studies Centre.

Channel 4 Television (2000), *Slavery: Commodities and Disposable People in the Modern World*.

Earth Letter (various), publication of Earth Ministry.

Economist, The (various).

Energy Saving Trust literature.

Environmental Justice Foundation (2003), *Squandering the Seas*.

Ethical Consumer, The (various).

Fairtrade Foundation literature.

Food and Agriculture Association (2003), *State of the World's Fisheries and Aquaculture 2002.*

Friends of the Earth information booklets: *Disappearing Forests, Energy and Climate Change, Our Threatened Wildlife, Waste, Road Transport and Air Pollution, Water Pollution.*

—— *Earth Matters* (FoE supporters' magazine) (various).

—— (1999), *Real Food: Time to Choose.*

—— (n.d.), *Don't Throw It All Away: Friends of the Earth's Guide to Waste Reduction and Recyling.*

Gott, C., and Johnston, K. (for the Home Office Research, Development and Statistics Directorate) (2000), *The Migrant Population in the UK: Fiscal Effects.*

International Action Against Child Poverty (IAACP) (2002), *Grow Up Free from Poverty: Meeting the 2015 Targets: A Progress Report.*

Kura, Y., Burke, L., McAllister, D., and Kassem, K. (2000), 'The Impact of Global Trawling: Mapping our Footprint on the Seafloor', from EarthTrends, the World Resources Institute website: <earthtrends.wri.org>.

London Institute for Contemporary Christianity/Administry (n.d.), *Supporting Christians at Work.*

Marine Conservation Society factsheets on chemical pollution, marine litter, nutrient pollution, climate change, sewage pollution, oil pollution, plastics and radioactive pollution.

Mills, P. (1990), 'Interest in Interest: The Relevance of the Old Testament Ban on Interest for Today', Cambridge Papers 2/1.

—— (1995), 'Faith *versus* Prudence? Christians and Financial Security', Cambridge Papers 4/1.

—— (1996), 'Investing as a Christian: Reaping Where You Have Not Sown?', Cambridge Papers 5/2.

Mock, G., White, R., and Wagener, A. (2001), 'Farming Fish: The Aquaculture Boom', from EarthTrends, the World Resources Institute website: <earthtrends.wri.org>.

Myers, N. (1997), 'Environmental Refugees', taken from *Population and Environment: A Journal of Interdisciplinary Studies* 19/2. Supplied by the Refugee Studies Centre.

New Internationalist, The (various).

Oxfam Policy Paper (2000), 'Globalization'.

Racial Justice Sunday Packs, 2001 and 2002.

Rainforest Action Network literature.

Refugee Action (2002), *Is It Safe Here? Refugee Women's Experiences in the UK*.

Revenga, C. (2000), 'Will There be Enough Water?', from EarthTrends, the World Resources Institute website: <earthtrends.wri.org>.

Revenga, C., and Mock, G. (2000), 'Dirty Water: Pollution Problems Persist', from EarthTrends, the World Resources Institute website: <earthtrends.wri.org>.

—— (2000), 'Freshwater Biodiversity in Crisis', from EarthTrends, the World Resources Institute website: <earthtrends.wri.org>.

Save the Children material.

Soil Association, *Living Earth* (member magazine) (various).

—— (2001), *The Truth About Food*.

—— (2001), 'No such thing as a free lunch in salmon farming: MSPs asked to steer clear of slap-up salmon dinner' (press release).

—— (2002), *Pesticides Allowed under SA and UKROFS Organic Standards* (SA Briefing Paper).

—— (2002), *Lindane and Breast Cancer: Why Take Risks?* (SA Policy Paper).

Southwark Diocese (2000), *Bishop's Report into Institutional Racism*.

Tearfund (2000), *A Tearfund Guide to Tourism: Don't Forget Your Ethics!*

—— (2000), *A Tearfund Guide to Water: Water in Tomorrow's World*.

—— (2002), *A Tearfund Guide to Child Prostitution: Trade in Human Misery*.

—— (2002), *Worlds Apart: A Call to Responsible Global Tourism*.

—— (n.d.), *Water Matters*.

UNEP (United Nations Environment Programme), 'Vital Water Graphics: Executive Summary', from the UNEP website, <www.unep.org>.

UNICEF (2000), *Unicef Annual Report*.

—— (2001), *Unicef Annual Report*.

—— (2002), *Unicef Annual Report*.

Valerio, R. (2002a), 'Globalization and Poverty' (Cred Paper). (Provides further bibliography on globalization.)
—— (2002b), 'Simplicity: Living Life to the Full' (Cred Paper).
Waterways Trust literature.
World Development Movement (1998), *The Good Life: Your Guide to Everyday Actions which Ensure a Fairer Deal for the World's Poor.*

Notes

Full details of works cited below are provided in the Bibliography.

Introduction

1 To read more about the history of evangelical social and political action, see J. Wolfe (ed.), *Evangelical Faith and Public Zeal*.
2 J. Stott (ed.), *Making Christ Known*, pp. 181–182.
3 Taken from the 1967 National Evangelical Anglican Congress, cited in J. Stott, *Issues Facing Christians Today*, p. 10.
4 To look further at these issues, see V. Samuel and C. Sugden (eds.), *Mission as Transformation*, and J. Stott, *Issues Facing Christians Today*, ch. 1.
5 One excellent resource is Christian Aid's *Act Justly*, which is designed to help small groups think and act biblically on world issues.

A is for Activists

1 J. A. Motyer, *The Prophecy of Isaiah*, p. 461.
2 Motyer, *The Prophecy of Isaiah*, pp. 478–482.
3 See further Rom. 8:19–21; 2 Cor. 5:18–21; Eph. 2:11–18; Col. 1:19–20.
4 Matt. 11:5; 25:31ff. and Luke 1:46–55 are all further expressions of what Jesus came to do.
5 C. J. H. Wright, *Living as the People of God*, pp. 82–83.
6 *The New Internationalist* (November 2001), p. 19.
7 2002 Report from the New Policy Institute (with support from the Joseph Rowntree Foundation).
8 J. Moltmann, *Theology of Hope*, p. 2.
9 P. Kuzmic, 'Eschatology and Ethics: Evangelical Views and Attitudes', in V. Samuel and C. Sugden (eds.), *Mission as Transformation*, p. 151.
10 Kuzmic, 'Eschatology and Ethics', p. 151, citing Bruce Milne, *What the Bible Teaches About the End of the World* (Wheaton, IL: Tyndale, 1982), p. 146.
11 CAFOD, Christian Aid and Tearfund all produce helpful prayer material that can help our prayers maintain a global focus.

B is for Bananas

1 Fairtrade Foundation.
2 Much of the following information on bananas comes from *The New Internationalist* (October 1999).
3 Also well known is Fyffes, which is the fifth-biggest company (after the Ecuadorian Noboa). Fyffes has about 8% of world trade. It is number two

in the EU market and may become number one in 2004, supplying about 21% of the 4 million tonnes consumed in the EU.

4 *Slavery: Commodities and Disposable People in the Modern World*, Channel 4 Television. Since the Channel 4 programme, the cocoa and chocolate industry have begun to put in place measures to combat abusive child or forced labour. For more details see <www.chocolateandcocoa.org>.

5 All coffee information comes from *The Ethical Consumer* (October/ November 2001).

6 Fairtrade Foundation.

7 Sainsbury's has also worked with the Fairtrade Foundation to develop its 'own label' range of FT goods, including coffee, tea and chocolate.

8 Ethical Trading Initiative, *Annual Report* (2001/2002).

9 Taken from the Base Code of Labour of the Ethical Trading Initiative.

10 There is not the space here to look in detail at how these organizations are set up and run. For more information, see J. Stiglitz, *Globalization and Its Discontents*, and the excellent resources that can be obtained from the World Development Movement, Oxfam and Christian Aid. See also the relevant websites: <www.wto.org>; <www.imf.org>; <www.worldbank.org>.

11 Taken from Christian Aid's 'Trade for life' material.

12 The Trade Justice Movement gives us the opportunity to do exactly that. It is a coalition of organizations campaigning to see these changes take place so that trade works for everyone. It brings together aid agencies, environment and human-rights campaigns, FT organizations and faith and consumer groups. For more information see <www.tradejusticemovement.org.uk>.

C is for Creation

1 For more on this, see C. J. H. Wright, *Living as the People of God*, pp. 68–69.

2 L. Osborn, *Guardians of Creation*, p. 29. See, for example, the descriptions of kingship given in Jer. 22:15–16 and 1 Kgs. 12:7.

3 The view that Christianity is guilty of domination over creation was famously proposed by Dr Lynn White in a 1967 article in *Nature* entitled 'The Historical Roots of our Ecologic Crisis'.

4 Taken from ch. 4 ('Ecology and the Earth') of the forthcoming revised edition of C. J. H. Wright, *Living as the People of God*.

5 W. J. Dumbrell, *Covenant and Creation*, p. 34, and also C. J. H. Wright, 'Ecology and the Earth'.

6 C. J. H. Wright, 'Ecology and the Earth' (italics his).

7 E.g. Deut. 30:15–16; Is. 5:8–10; Jer. 5:23–25.

8 2 Cor. 5:18–21; Eph. 2:11–18; Rom. 8:19–22.

9 C. Gunton, *Christ and Creation*, p. 64.

10 For more on this see R. Valerio, 'Chainsaws, Planes and Komodo Dragons: Globalization and the Environment', in R. Tiplady (ed.), *One World or Many?*.

11 This is of course based on the 'first fruits' of Jesus' resurrection body, which demonstrates both continuity and discontinuity with his old body and is both physical and spiritual as he eats fish yet walks through walls.

12 D. Wilkinson, *The Message of Creation*, p. 261.

13 R. Bauckham and T. Hart, *Hope Against Hope*, p. 137.

D is for Driving

1 Much of the information for this chapter comes from Friends of the Earth's paper, *Road Transport and Air Pollution*, and from *The Ecologist, Go M.A.D!*

2 *The Ethical Consumer* (December 2000/January 2001), p. 10.

3 West Sussex County Council, *Connections* magazine (summer 2001).

4 D. McClaren, S. Bullock and N. Yousuf, *Tomorrow's World*, pp. 117–118. Statistic on average car costs comes from the RAC.

5 McClaren et al., *Tomorrow's World*, p. 113.

6 Phone 01323 417700 or visit <www.powerplus.be> for more details.

E is for Energy

1 For more on this see 'W is for Water'.

2 D. McClaren, S. Bullock and N. Yousuf, *Tomorrow's World*, p. 85.

3 *The New Internationalist* (June 2001), p. 12.

4 Southern Sudan is another place where people's lives are being ruined because of fighting around oil (for more details contact Christian Aid); and the planned Baku–Tbilisi–Ceyhan pipeline in eastern Europe looks set to stir up plenty of controversy (contact Friends of the Earth for more details).

5 McClaren et al., *Tomorrow's World*, p. 86.

6 Cited in M. Northcott, *Life After Debt*, p. 66.

7 To look at this further, see my Tearfund Policy Paper, *A Biblical Perspective on Globalization*.

8 Friends of the Earth, *Energy and Climate Change*, p. 5.

9 See also Ps. 104 and Job 38 – 42.

10 *The Ecologist, Go M.A.D!*, p. 57.

11 For further ideas get hold of Tearfund's action paper on *Climate Change*.

F is for Food

1 Eccles. 3:1–8; Ps. 1:3.

2 This contrasts with only four pesticides that are allowed under the Soil Association's standards: soft soap, sulphur and copper (which are from traditional use in organic farming) and rotenone, which is of natural origin (Soil Association Briefing Paper, *Pesticides Allowed Under SA and UKROFS Organic Standards*).

3 For more information on Lindane see the Soil Association's policy paper, *Lindane and Breast Cancer: Why Take Risks?*

4 I am concentrating on vegetables and fruit here, but the same can, of course, also be said of meat with the little-known dangers of eating animals that have been regularly given antibiotics and are themselves eating feeds that contains pesticides.

5 Soil Association, *The Truth About Food.*

6 For more on this see J. Humphrys, *The Great Food Gamble*, ch. 1.

7 *The Ecologist, Go M.A.D!*, p. 60.

8 I am not going to cover GM foods in this book. For more information contact Friends of the Earth and the Soil Association, and see Humphrys, *The Great Food Gamble*, ch. 8.

9 Soil Association, *The Truth About Food.*

10 M. Van Straten, *Organic Living*, p. 31.

11 H. Fearnley-Whittingstall, *The River Cottage Cookbook*, p. 209: a fantastically inspiring book.

12 For more on salmon, see 'K is for Kippers'. Eating wild salmon is not an alternative, as stocks are dwindling. The only way to be sure that the salmon you are eating was not reared in an environmentally detrimental way is to source it from an organic farm.

13 A recent development in farming is a move towards 'integrated farm management', a system of farming that includes the use of traditional techniques along with modern pesticides and that aims to minimize environmental impact. Their view is that pesticides contribute importantly to our health and quality of life by, for example, enabling crops to be produced more efficiently, reducing the contamination of food by toxic fungi, and controlling insects that spread human diseases. Recognizing their potential dangers, however, their approach is that one should 'use as much pesticide as is necessary to do the job, but as little as possible'. For more details, contact the Crop Protection Association UK at <www.cropprotection.org.uk> and the British Crop Protection Council at <www.bcpc.org>.

14 The National Farmers' Union.

15 Friends of the Earth, *Real Food: Time to Choose'*, pp. 6–7.

16 W. Berry, 'The Pleasures of Eating', in M. Schut (ed.), *Simpler Living, Compassionate Life*, p. 106.

17 For one attempt to enhance the relationship between food and time, see <www.slowfood.com>.

18 M. Schut, 'Food as Sacrament', in *Earth Letter* (November 2001), p. 11.

G is for Globalization

1 My writing on globalization started in the form of three Tearfund Policy Papers: *Globalization and the Poor*; *Globalization, the Church and Mission* and *A Biblical Perspective on Globalization*. The material in this

chapter draws on those papers and on other writing and speaking that I have done on this subject, including two chapters in Tiplady, *One World or Many?*. My fullest writing on globalization is now in the form of a Cred Paper entitled *Globalization and Poverty*. To obtain a copy contact Cred (see 'A is for Activists' for details).

2 I. Linden, in C. Reed (ed.), *Development Matters*, p. 3.

3 Department for International Development report on globalization, *Eliminating Poverty: Making Globalization Work for the Poor.*

4 LEB, p. 81.

5 M. Moore, 'Trade Rules for Global Commerce', *Global Future* (First Quarter, 2001), p. 2.

6 'Of Celebrities, Charities and Trade', *The Economist* (1 June 2002).

7 The UK Department for International Development would be an excellent example of a body taking this view.

8 For two excellent defences of globalization see J. Micklethwaite and A. Wooldridge, *A Future Perfect*, and P. Legrain, *Open World.*

9 One of the key voices on this side is Joseph Stiglitz (see his *Globalization and Its Discontents*).

10 N. Klein (2000), *No Logo*, London: Flamingo.

11 To look at this further, see Stiglitz, *Globalization and Its Discontents.*

12 See Legrain, *Open World.*

13 P. Heslam, *Globalization*, p. 25.

14 I am aware of the dangers of putting future scenarios into print. By the time this gets published the world scene may have changed again.

15 This reform would include eliminating unequal voting rights, allowing flexibility in policies and preventing the development of trade rules that stop national governments pursuing the right policies for development.

16 Underlying both of these is the need to deal with corruption and bring in internationally recognized anti-corruption laws.

17 See also Rev. 5:9–10; 11:15; 21:22–26; 22:1–3.

18 This point is made by S. Escobar, 'The Global Scenario at the Turn of the Century', in W. Taylor (ed.), *Global Missiology for the Twenty-first Century.*

19 A. Araujo, 'Globalization and World Evangelism', in Taylor (ed.), *Global Missiology*, p. 60. Dewi Hughes has also reminded me here that globalization has potentially benefited world evangelization, since technology has made it very difficult for any government to prevent its citizens hearing the gospel.

H is for HIV

1 *The New Internationalist* (December 1993), p. 18.

2 Unless otherwise stated, the statistics in this chapter come from UNAIDS' 'Aids Epidemic Update' (December 2001).

3 G. Paterson, 'HIV/Aids: A Window on Development', in C. Reed (ed.), *Development Matters*, p. 45.

4 Acet UK, 'HIV/Aids Update' (July 2000).
5 *The New Internationalist* (December 1993), p. 13.
6 Paterson, 'HIV/Aids', p. 45.
7 Paterson, 'HIV/Aids', p. 46.
8 Acet UK, 'HIV/Aids Update' (July 2000).
9 C. von Ruhland, *Louder than Words*, p. 4.
10 Taken from the World Corner website, <www.world-corner.org>.
11 My thanks to Adrian Gosling, Director of HopeHIV, for these points.

I is for Investments

1 Taken from Triodosnews (editions 8 and 9).
2 The material in the following paragraphs comes from P. Mills, 'Faith *versus* Prudence?'
3 P. Mills, 'Investing as a Christian', has been invaluable here.
4 To look further at this, see P. Mills, 'Interest in Interest'.
5 See Mills, 'Investing as a Christian', for a helpful look at the current investment options in the light of some of these principles.
6 I feel duty-bound at this point to mention the risk element involved in all investments in general. Sometimes we shall lose money through them rather than make it.
7 This is not an exhaustive list. EIRIS can provide a fuller list of financial products.

J is for Jobs

1 J. Dominguez and V. Robin (*Your Money or Your Life*, pp. 229–230) would go further. They state that the only purpose served by paid employment is getting paid, and stress that the other personal aspects are all equally available in unpaid activities.
2 Quoted in J. Luhrs, *The Simple Living Guide*.
3 M. Greene, 'Supporting Christians at Work (without going insane)', p. 13, citing the '1999 Survey of Managers' Changing Experiences' from the Institute of Management.
4 P. A. Marshall, 'Work', in D. J. Atkinson et al. (eds.), *New Dictionary of Christian Ethics and Pastoral Theology*, p. 900.
5 J. Stott, *Issues Facing Christians Today*, p. 166.
6 P. A. Marshall, 'Work', p. 899.
7 M. Greene, 'Supporting Christians at Work'.

K is for Kippers

1 Y. Kura, L. Burke, D. McAllister and K. Kassem, 'The Impact of Global Trawling'.
2 Environmental Justice Foundation, *Squandering the Seas*.
3 The following two chapters are taken from the Marine Conservation Society's factsheets.

4 It is interesting to note that oil spills account for less than 10% of oil pollution. Most of it comes from spillages at oil terminals, installations and coastal refineries, and from routine tank-cleaning that deliberately releases oil into the sea.

5 Food and Agriculture Organization (FAO).

6 FAO, 'State of the World's Fisheries and Aquaculture 2002'.

7 For a good account of the effects of salmon farming, see the chapter on 'Fear of Fish: Fish Farming', in J. Humphrys, *The Great Food Gamble*.

8 Soil Association press release, 'No such thing as a free lunch in salmon farming'.

9 This paragraph comes from G. Mock, R. White and A. Wagener, 'Farming Fish: The Aquaculture Boom', p. 3.

L is for Letters

1 Since writing this the supermarket chain agreed to stock FT bananas in their London stores as a trial and have now announced that they are putting them into all their shops – a direct result of consumer pressure.

2 Union leader in the Dominican Republic, campaigned for by Amnesty International.

3 Rainforest Action Network and Friends of the Earth will provide information on all of this.

M is for Money

1 Some of this material also appears in J. Odgers and R. Valerio, *Simplicity, Love and Justice*.

2 C. Blomberg, *Neither Poverty Nor Riches*, p. 83.

3 D. Kraybill, *The Upside-down Kingdom*, pp. 114–129.

4 *The Message* paraphrase of the Bible gives an excellent re-reading of this passage.

5 Thanks to Phil Wall for this idea.

N is for Needs

1 Brian Rosner describes our culture as following a 'religion of greed' in *How to Get Really Rich*.

2 Bishop James Jones makes the point that 'Christianity is a religion of consumption. We are natural and original consumers. The Garden of Eden is planted with food for us to eat. And when the founder of Christianity departed this life he gave his followers an act of consumption by which to remember him.' James Jones, *Jesus and the Earth*, p. 25.

3 T. Sine and C. Sine, *Living on Purpose*, pp. 138–139.

4 Sine, *Living on Purpose*, p. 40.

5 N. T. Wright, *For All God's Worth*.

6 Sine, *Living on Purpose*, p. 32.

7 These come from J. Odgers and R. Valerio, *Simplicity, Love and Justice*.

O is for Organic

1 This needn't always be the case; some dairy products are now so popular that they cost the same as non-organic, and local veg box delivery schemes are often cheaper than organic produce from the supermarkets.

2 The following material comes from *Living Earth*, the magazine of the Soil Association (April/June 2002).

3 *Earth Matters*, the magazine of Friends of the Earth (autumn 2000), p. 13.

4 A good book to start you off is G. Hamilton, *The Organic Garden Book*.

5 Down to Earth and Ecover both provide a full range of cleaning products.

6 For recipes for both cleaning products and beauty products (and a whole host of other organic things), check out <www.care2.com>, a great website.

7 *The Ethical Consumer* (April/May 2002), p. 16.

8 Culpeper (<www.culpeper.co.uk>), Green People (<www.greenpeople.co.uk>), Logona (<logona.co.uk>), Neal's Yard (<nealsyardremedies.com>) and Weleda (<www.weleda.co.uk>) are all good companies to look at.

9 M. Van Straten, *Organic Living*, p. 15.

P is for Paper

1 Unless otherwise indicated, all the information in this chapter comes from Rainforest Action Network factsheets.

2 *The Ecologist, Go M.A.D!*, p. 110.

3 Friends of the Earth, *Disappearing Forests*, pp. 2–3.

4 C. Reed (ed.) (2001), *Development Matters: Christian Perspectives on Globalisation*, London: Church House Publishing, p. 54.

5 Friends of the Earth, *Disappearing Forests*, p. 10. for more information on how to buy 'good wood', see the *Good Wood Guide* from Friends of the Earth.

6 For more information check out <www.mcspotlight.org>.

R is for Recyling

1 Unless otherwise stated, the material for this chapter all comes from Friends of the Earth literature.

2 *The Ecologist, Go M.A.D!*, p. 155. In England and Wales, between 1983/4 and 1999/2000 the amount of household waste increased by a third (DEFRA).

3 DEFRA.

4 *The Ecologist, Go M.A.D!*, p. 155.

5 This research was published in the medical journal the *Lancet* (8 August 1998), pp. 423–427). For more information, see <www.foe.co.uk/pubsinfo/infoteam/pressrel/1998/19980807122119.html>.

6 Quoted in J. Odgers and R. Valerio, *Simplicity, Love and Justice*, p. 52.

7 Natracare: 0117 946 6649. For more information on all of this, including

re-usable sanitary protection, contact the Women's Environmental
Network: 0171 247 3327.
8   *The Ecologist, Go M.A.D!*, p. 101.
9   *The Ecologist, Go M.A.D!*, p. 157.
10 For more details on all of these, see Friends of the Earth, *Don't Throw it
    all Away.*
11 <www.wastepoint.co.uk> or <www.recycle-more.com> are good sites to
    visit.
12 *The Ecologist, Go M.A.D!*, p. 155.

S is for Simplicity

1   The bulk of this chapter is based on material in J. Odgers and R. Valerio,
    Simplicity, Love and Justice.
2   T. Sine, *Mustard Seed versus McWorld*, p. 128.
3   R. McCloughry, 'Community Ethics', in D. J. Atkinson et al. (eds.), *New
    Dictionary of Christian Ethics and Pastoral Theology*, p. 110.
4   M. Schut (ed.), *Simpler Living, Compassionate Life*, p. 253.
5   It has been pointed out to me that alongside silence, solitude and
    contemplation stand the complementary triad of intercession,
    community and the Word of God. I find this helpful and hope that these
    are reflected elsewhere in the book.
6   Schut (ed.), *Simpler Living, Compassionate Life*, pp. 50–51. If you want
    to take this a step further, I recommend R. Foster, *Prayer.*
7   Henri Nouwen, 'Contemplation and Ministry', in Schut (ed.), *Simpler
    Living, Compassionate Life*, p. 54.
8   R. Foster, *Freedom of Simplicity*, pp. 8–9.
9   Foster, *Freedom of Simplicity*, p. 14.

T is for Tourism

1   This depends on the world situation. In times of war, or increased
    instability, the arms trade is the biggest industry.
2   World Tourist Organization (WTO). 'Tourist arrivals' is the term used to
    measure tourism.
3   Association of British Travel Agents.
4   Tearfund, *Worlds Apart.*
5   *Worlds Apart*, citing WTO statistics.
6   These countries are Brazil, China, Ethiopia, India, Indonesia, Kenya,
    Mexico, Nepal, Nigeria, Peru, Philippines. *Worlds Apart*, citing C. Ashley,
    Pro-Poor Tourism Strategies: Making Tourism Work for the Poor
    (Overseas Development Institute, 2001).
7   For more details on this see the 'responsible tourism' page on their
    website, <www.abta.com>, and read their paper: ABTA and Tearfund,
    'Improving Tour Operator Performance: The Role of Corporate Social
    Responsibility and Reporting'.

8 See <www.responsibletravel.com>. For details of other initiatives, and case studies, see <www.toinitiative.org>.

9 Tourism Concern leaflet.

10 *The Observer* (27 October 2001).

11 Tourism Concern website. TC has been at the front of raising awareness of tourism issues.

12 For more details on A Rocha's work, see their contact details in 'C is for Creation'.

13 Tourism concern leaflet.

14 Research from Brunel University, cited in Tourism Concern, *In Focus* (winter 1996).

15 John Spellar MP, Transport Minister (9 April 2002).

16 For more details on being 'carbon neutral' contact Climate Care.

17 ABTA Package Holidays Survey (2002).

U is for Unwanted Peoples

1 The 1951 Geneva Refugee Convention.

2 UNHCR, *Statistical Yearbook 2001*, p. 12.

3 Europe hosts 2.2 million and America 650,000 (UNHCR, *Statistical Yearbook 2001*). This chapter is focusing on refugees from a global perspective, and we shall consider the UK perspective regarding asylum-seekers in 'X is for Xenophobia'.

4 UNHCR, *Statistical Yearbook 2001*, p. 13.

5 Save the Children, Liberia Emergency Update (September 2002).

6 N. Myers, 'Environmental Refugees', pp. 167–168. While these are the figures generally stated, there is debate over the extent of the environmental refugee problem among governments and aid agencies and in academia. To read the other side, see R. Black, 'Environmental Refugees: Myth or Reality?'

7 UNHCR, 'Basic Information about UNHCR', from website: <www.unhcr.ch>.

8 UNHCR, 'World Refugee Overview' (from website).

9 Oxfam, 'Asylum Facts', from website: <www.oxfam.org.uk>.

10 Save the Children, 'War brought us here: protecting children displaced within their own countries by conflict' (2000).

11 UNHCR, *Statistical Yearbook 2001*, p. 13.

12 Oxfam, 'Asylum Facts'.

13 Oxfam, 'Asylum Facts'.

14 See 'A is for Activists'.

V is for Volunteers

1 Institute for Volunteering Research, 'The 1997 National Survey of Volunteering'. 48% of adults engage in formal volunteering. The financial calculation is based on figures in the 1997 Survey.

2 For more details of these and others, see the 'Residential Volunteering Opportunities in the UK' paper produced by the National Centre for Volunteering.
3 For more information on gap years, see <www.studentvol.org.uk>; <www.gap.org.uk>; <www.gapyear.com>.
4 For more information see the 'Volunteering overseas' paper produced by the National Centre for Volunteering.
5 Taken from *TimeGuide*, published by TimeBank in association with the National Centre for Volunteering, p. 13. For more information, see <www.volunteering.org.uk/Eitcn> (Employees in the Community Network); <www.bitc.org.uk> (Business in the Community) and <www.csv.org> (Community Service Volunteers).
6 Taken from the 1997 National Survey of Volunteering.
7 *The Ecologist, Go M.A.D!*, p. 152.
8 These questions are taken from R. McCloughry, *Taking Action*, p. 23, and from *TimeGuide*, p. 6.

W is for Water
1 C. Revenga, 'Will There be Enough Water?', taken from the EarthTrends website, <earthtrends.wri.org>, using figures from the World Resources Institute in collaboration with the University of New Hampshire. An area in 'water stress' is one that is subject to frequent water shortages.
2 UNEP, 'Vital Water Graphics: Executive Summary', taken from the UNEP website, <www.unep.org>.
3 UNEP, 'Vital Water Graphics'.
4 C. Revenga, 'Will There be Enough Water?'. Drip irrigation systems can cut water use by as much as 70%, while simultaneously increasing crop yields.
5 Tearfund, 'Water Matters' campaign material.
6 See 'T is for Tourism'.
7 In Africa it is estimated that twenty-five countries will be experiencing water stress by 2025 (UNEP, 'Vital Water Graphics').
8 *The Ecologist, Go M.A.D!*, p. 158.
9 D. McLaren, S. Bullock and N. Yousuf, *Tomorrow's World*, pp. 185–186.
10 McLaren, Bullock and Yousuf, *Tomorrow's World*, pp. 188–189.
11 A 'large' dam is higher than 15 m or impounds more than 3 million m^3 of water.
12 C. Revenga and G. Mock, 'Freshwater Biodiversity in Crisis', taken from the EarthTrends website.
13 UNEP, 'Vital Water Graphics', nos. 24, 25, 26, 27.
14 UNEP, 'Vital Water Graphics'.
15 C. Revenga and G. Mock, 'Dirty Water'.
16 Friends of the Earth, 'Water Pollution' (1998); Revenga and Mock, 'Dirty Water'.

17 For more information on these and other ideas, contact the organizations listed at the end of this chapter.

18 'Other' uses 16% and external use is 5% (McLaren, Bullock and Yousuf, *Tomorrow's World*, p. 196).

X is for Xenophobia

1 Phoenix Community Care can be contacted at 72 Palmerston Road, Wood Green, London N22 8RF; 020 8808 8000.

2 D. Haslam, *Race for the Millennium*, p. 210.

3 This can be seen also in the growing popularity of the British National Party. Although still a decidedly minority party, it did have four elected councillors in 2002.

4 National Statistics, 'Minority Ethnic Groups in the UK' (2002), p. 1.

5 National Statistics, 'Minority Ethnic Groups', p. 2.

6 National Statistics, 'Minority Ethnic Groups', p. 3.

7 A campaign for justice for Mal and Linda is being run by local anti-racists, the Churches' Commission for Racial Justice and the Friends of Mal Hussain (established by the National Assembly Against Racism). For more details, contact Friends of Mal Hussain, c/o NAAR, 28 Commercial St, London E1 6LS.

8 The European Monitoring Centre on Racism and Xenophobia's report on Racism and Cultural Diversity in the Mass Media. See <www.eucm.at/publications>.

9 Refugee Council, 'Nailing press myths about refugees, introduction' (2002), taken from website, <www.refugeecouncil.org.uk/news/myths/myth001.htm>. This article by the Refugee Council is a helpful challenge to some of the most common negative assumptions made by the media.

10 Haslam, *Race for the Millennium*, p. 201.

11 This paragraph is taken from the 'Frequently Asked Questions' on the Refugee Council's website.

12 For more details see the Refugee Council website's FAQs: 'Is the asylum system as fair as people say it is?'

13 C. Gott and K. Johnston, *The Migrant Population in the UK: Fiscal Effects'*.

14 Refugee Action, *Is It Safe Here?*, p. 1.

15 From Racial Justice Sunday pack, 2002.

16 J. Sacks, *Faith in the Future*, 78.

17 An excellent example of the church acknowledging the inroads that racism has made, and taking steps to change that, is the report on institutional racism by Southwark Diocese.

Y is for Young people

1 From a presentation given by S. Gallimore, Head of Child Protection for East Sussex.

2 Information from Barnardo's literature (2001).

3 S. Gallimore.

4 This is happening, for example, with regards to school exclusion. Cornerstone Church in Swansea runs a highly effective programme working with young people identified as most likely to be excluded.

5 UNICEF, *The State of the World's Children 2000*, p. 68; UNICEF, *Annual Report 2000*, p. 4.

6 International Action Against Child Poverty (IAACP), *Grow Up Free from Poverty*, p. 31 (using UNAIDS' figures from 2001).

7 For more on this issue in general, see 'H is for HIV'.

8 UNICEF, *Annual Report 2000*, p. 4.

9 149 million children are malnourished (UNICEF, *The State of the World's Children 2002*, p. 80).

10 UNICEF, *State of the World's Children 2001*, pp. 68-69. Encouragingly, UNICEF reported in 2002 that exclusive breastfeeding of 0-3-month-olds and the use of iodized salt in developing countries is increasing (*State of the World's Children 2002*, p. 78).

11 UNICEF, *State of the World's Children 2002*, p. 80.

12 UNICEF, *State of the World's Children 2001*, pp. 72, 92.

13 UNICEF, *State of the World's Children 2001*, pp. 70-71. In Burkino Faso and the Niger a shocking 90% of women are illiterate (*State of the World's Children 2000*, p. 72).

14 More than 2 million children died, and over 1 million children were orphaned or separated from their familes, in the last ten years as a direct result of armed conflict; and an estimated 300,000 children are serving in armed forces, as soldiers and servants, many being forced into sexual slavery. Each year about 6,000 children are killed or injured by landmines (UNICEF, *Annual Report 2000*, p. 14; *State of the World's Children* 2002, p. 42).

15 About a million children (mostly girls) are caught up in the commercial sex trade (UNICEF, *State of the World's Children 2002*), while 250 million children in developing countries work, many in hazardous and exploitative labour. Basic rights are often overlooked (UNICEF, *State of the World's Children 2000*, p. 74). Ninety per cent of domestic workers (the largest group of child workers in the world) are girls between 12 and 17 years old (UNICEF, *State of the World's Children 2002*, p. 52).

Z is for Zeitgeist

1 'Zeitgeist: New wave club culture' (Stress Recordings), 1997.

2 B. Goudzwaard, *Globalization and the Kingdom of God*, p. 68.

3 As in 'C is for Creation', 'G is for Globalization' and 'W is for Water'.

4 For more on this see N. T. Wright, *New Heavens, New Earth*, p. 22.